Reframing Italian America

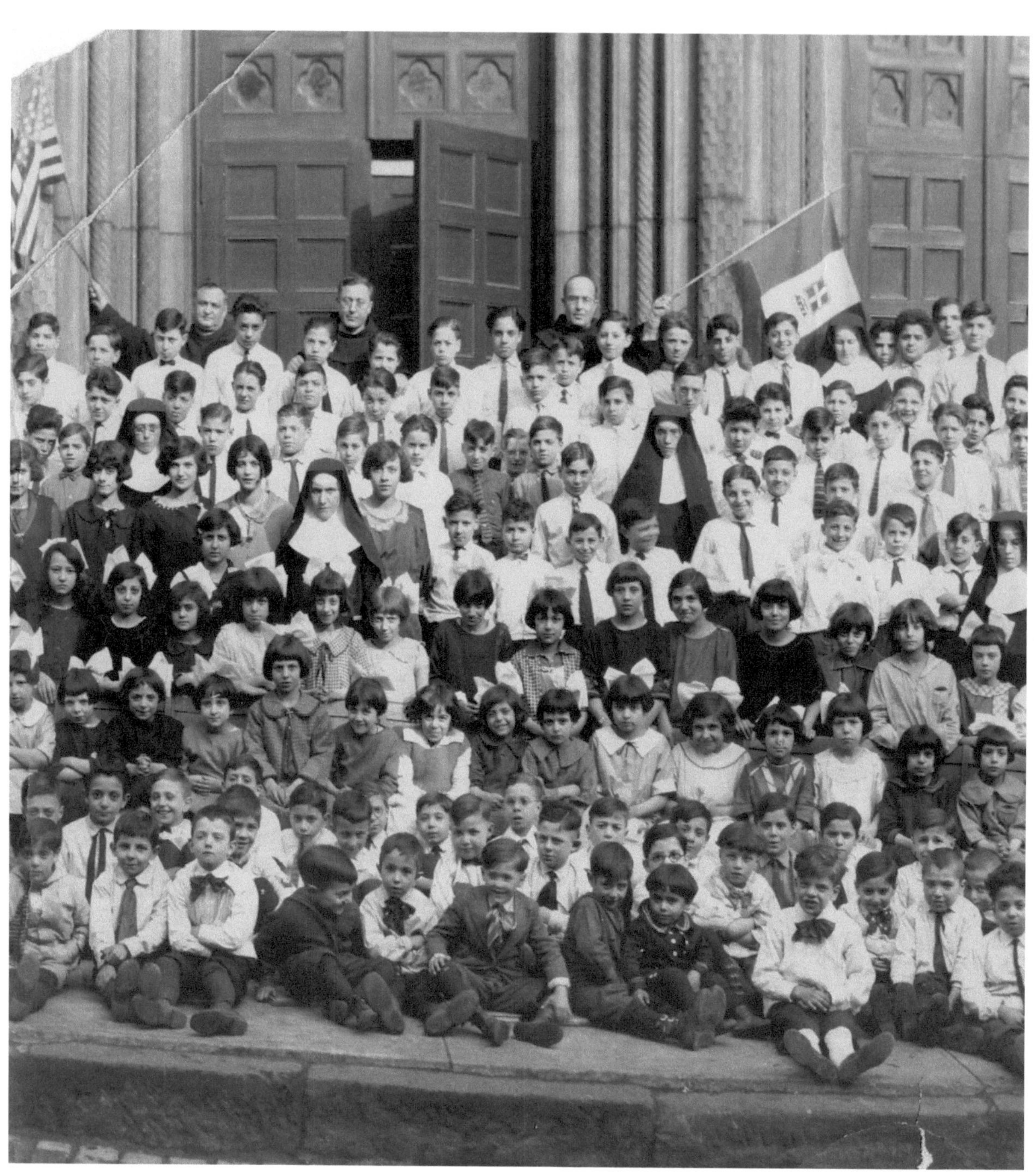

Reframing Italian America

HISTORICAL PHOTOGRAPHS AND IMMIGRANT REPRESENTATIONS

EDITED BY ROSANGELA BRISCESE AND JOSEPH SCIORRA

JOHN D. CALANDRA ITALIAN AMERICAN INSTITUTE

2015

Reframing Italian America

HISTORICAL PHOTOGRAPHS AND IMMIGRANT REPRESENTATIONS

STUDIES IN ITALIAN AMERICANA
VOLUME 11

Printed in the United States of America

John D. Calandra Italian American Institute
Queens College, CUNY
25 West 43rd Street, 17th floor
New York, NY 10036

ISBN 978-1-939323-07-1
Library of Congress Control Number: 2015939536

COVER
"Gruppo Cappellai Italiani" [Group of Italian Hatmakers]

FRONTISPIECE
Detail: St. Peter's Church, Fernando Street

Contents

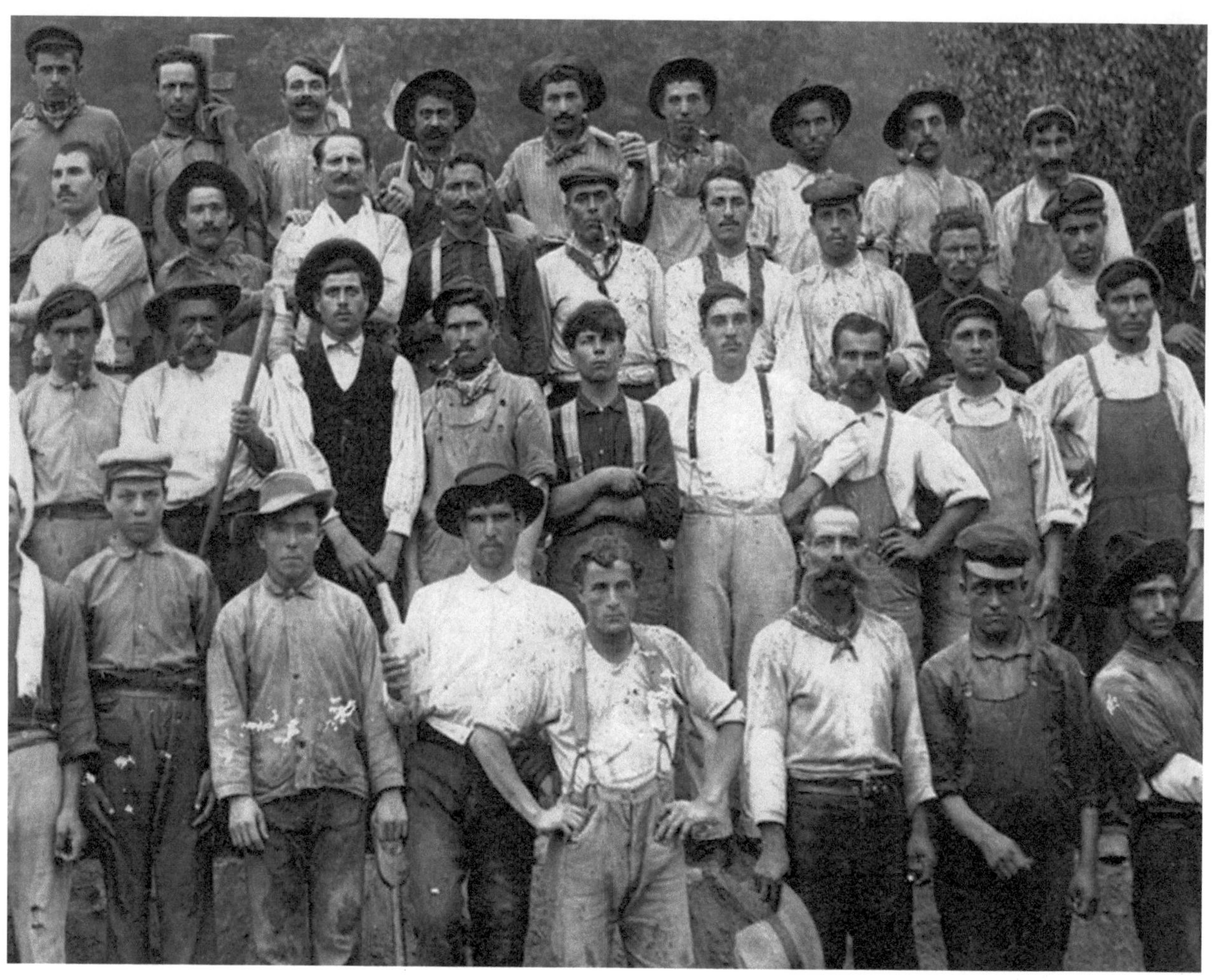

Detail: "Gruppo lavoratori Italiani" [Group of Italian workers]

Acknowledgments

WE WISH to express our gratitude to Michael Titowsky and Barbara Krysko, as well as to Mesrob Hratch Zadoian of Queens College, for their help in illuminating the life and work of Bernard Titowsky. It was a pleasure to work with Dominic DiPasquale, of DP Framing, who did a stunning job of framing the photographs for the exhibition. We are eternally grateful to designer Polly Franchini, of Oronzo Editions, whose generosity and skills in designing this publication know no bounds. Queens College student Vincent Rivera meticulously scanned the photographs included in this publication. Bibliophile James Periconi provided access to his copy of *Gli italiani negli Stati Uniti d'America*. The following individuals helped us identify some of the people and places depicted in the photographs: Tommaso Caiazza of the Ca' Foscari University of Venice; E. E. "Skip" Campbell of the Gadsden Center at the University of Alabama; Donna M. DeBlasio of the Center for Applied History at Youngstown State University; Mary Jo Fritts of the Italian American Heritage Society in Birmingham; Melissa E. Marinaro of the Italian American Program at the Senator John Heinz History Center; and Gretchen Stallone and Bianca de Mattia of the Margaret R. Grundy Memorial Library in Bristol, Pennsylvania. We thank Laura E. Ruberto for offering her insights to an earlier draft of Sciorra's essay and Siân Gibby of the Calandra Institute for closely reading and editing the book in its entirety. Finally, much praise goes to Anthony Julian Tamburri, who as the dean of the Calandra Institute understands the significance of ongoing research on the history and culture of Italian Americans and most importantly of providing the resources to Calandra Institute staff that make it possible for them to implement their best work.

Rosangela Briscese and Joseph Sciorra

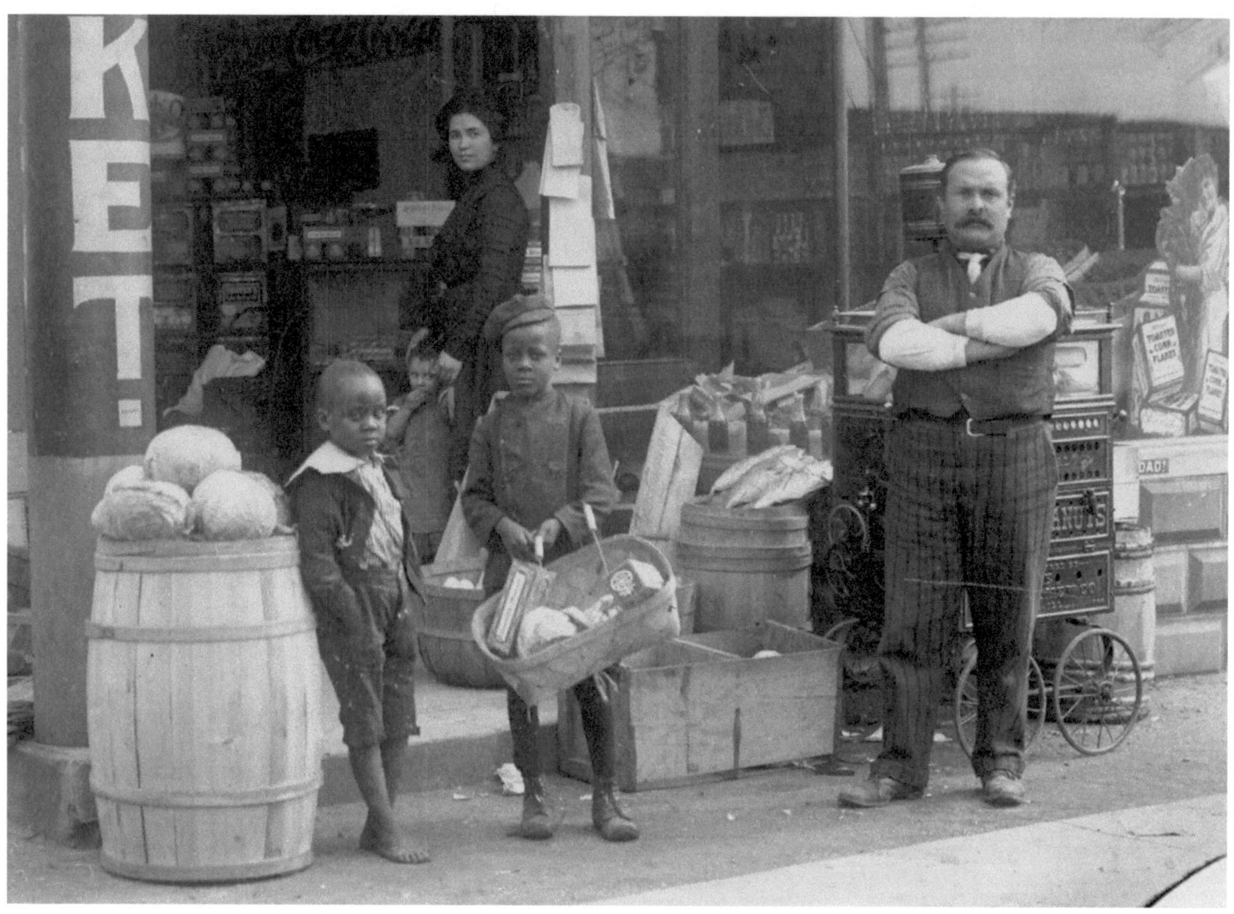

Detail: Pietro Giammusso, Italian Fruit Store

HISTORY OUT OF A SUITCASE

ITALIAN IMMIGRANT REPRESENTATION IN THE BERNARD TITOWSKY COLLECTION PHOTOGRAPHS

JOSEPH SCIORRA

IN 1999, attorney Michael Titowsky donated a suitcase filled with over two-hundred historical photographs to Queens College's John D. Calandra Italian American Institute, a City University of New York research institute dedicated to studying Italian-American history and culture. These items had been collected by his deceased father, Bernard Titowsky, a rare-book seller from Queens. Most of the photographs are undated and depict scenes and personalities of Italian immigrant life in the United States from approximately the first three decades of the twentieth century. A significant number of these prints are mounted on now-faded gray paperboard and captioned with meticulous and ornate calligraphy. In 2015, my Calandra Institute coworker Rosangela Briscese and I curated an exhibition of twenty-three of these photographs, selecting those that dealt specifically with Italian Americans and that were of both historical and aesthetic interest to us. The exhibition *Reframing Italian America: Historical Photographs and Immigrant Representations* ran from May 28, 2015, to January 8, 2016, in the Institute's Manhattan gallery. This book presents the twenty-three exhibited images (indicated in the catalog with an asterisk), plus an additional eighteen photos from the Titowsky Collection.

The purpose of making these images public via the exhibition and this book is to highlight the holdings of the Calandra Institute's archival collection while introducing a cache of historical images that appear to be otherwise unknown.[1] At the same time, given my conjecture (which I elaborate upon below) that a good number of these photographs were previously shown as part of an early-twentieth-century exhibit, possibly in Italy, *Reframing Italian America* also seeks to raise the question of how photography is enlisted to engender an imagined Italian community (pace Benedict Anderson) while contributing to what can be called a "national photography" (Verdicchio 2011, 1–7) vis-à-vis a diasporic frame of reference. The exhibition and book position these representations of migrant *italianità* (Italianness)—broadly defined to include commerce, labor, artistry, religion, and other fields of endeavor—as part of an ongoing attempt at "problematizing and undermining dominant narratives about nationally bounded culture and identity" (Sciorra 2015, xxvi) in a dialogic communication of visual materials.

Bernard Titowsky (1925–1993) was born in Brooklyn to illiterate Jewish parents who emigrated from Poland following World War I. He grew up in different neighborhoods, primarily Bensonhurst, and received his undergraduate degree from Queens College in 1947 and his master's degree in library science from the University of Wisconsin-Madison two years later. He went on to teach history and English in public high schools and junior high schools in Queens and was the librarian at John Bowne High School in Flushing; he retired sometime in the mid-1970s. In 1951, he married Rita Migliaccio, and they raised their two children, Michael and Barbara, in Kew Gardens, Queens. In 1964, he brought together his pedagogical experience and librarian's skills to write the book *American History: A Guide to Student Reading for Teachers and Librarians.*

Books were Titowsky's passion, especially those concerning U.S. history and immigration, and in 1954 he opened the Austin Book Shop at 82-60A Austin Street in Kew Gardens. Because of his day job, the retail store was open only on weekends. In time, it became a sort of neighborhood salon where locals gathered to discuss literature, politics, and other matters of the day. Michael Titowsky remembers:

> It became something of a hangout because a lot of his friends would just come over, and they would open up a couple of bottles of wine late in the afternoon and just kind of sit around and talk and drink and, you know, talk about books and things like that. So, it became something of a neighborhood hangout towards the end there. (Telephone interview, January 20, 2015)

Much of the shop's business was mail order, with Titowsky supplying university libraries and private collectors with out-of-print books. He would compile catalogs of his holdings to distribute to potential buyers such as the 1978 directory "Immigration & Ethnic Studies," with 888 annotated items. As part of his search for rare books, Titowsky also came across and purchased old photographs (including works by Lewis Hines), antique furniture, and other historical artifacts. According to his children, Titowsky was so successful with his business that the additional income allowed him to support his wife Rita as she attended law school (Telephone interview, January 20, 2015).

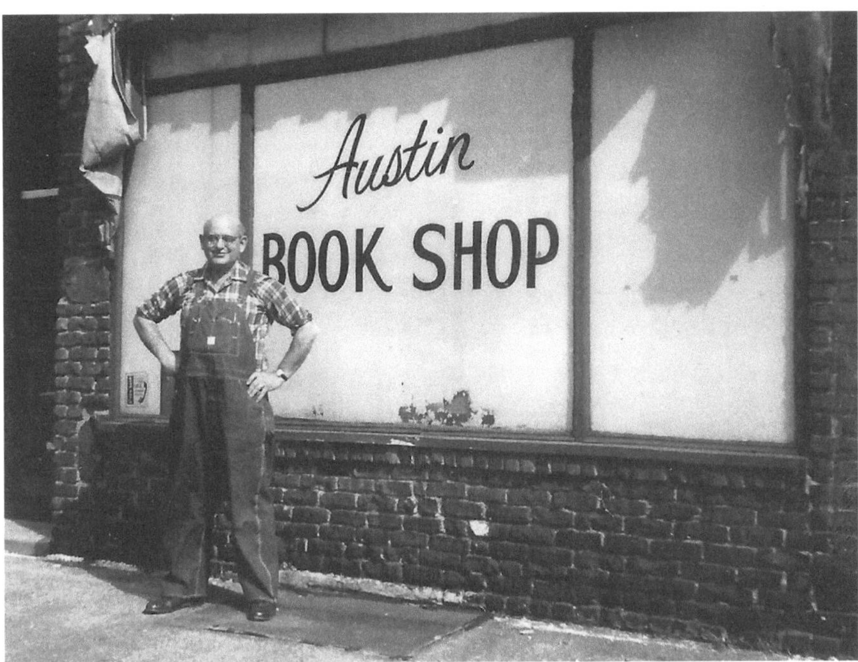

Bernard Titowsky standing in front of storage space on Austin Street, circa 1978.
Courtesy Barbara Krysko.

In 1970, Titowsky moved the retail part of the business around the corner to 82–60 Austin Street, eventually using 82–60A Austin Street exclusively for storage and shipping of mail-order purchases (Titowsky, "The Austin Book Shop—Part 1"). It is interesting to note that the original store became somewhat infamous as the site in front of which twenty-nine-year-old Catherine "Kitty" Genovese was first brutally attacked on March 13, 1964, eventually dying around the corner after a second attack. Two weeks later the *New York Times* ran a front-page story titled "37 Who Saw Murder Didn't Call Police," an account about apathy and anomie in the modern city that became international news. The story's implications had lasting repercussions for U.S. society as Americans reacted by forming block associations for safety, and university courses analyzed the disturbing new trend in U.S. society (Lemann 2014). The original newspaper story has since been severely criticized for its significant inaccuracies and for the damaging effects of the "thirty-eight witness myth" it created and perpetuated (Ibid.; see also Rasenberger 2004; Kaufman 2013). Twenty years after the vicious killing, Titowsky took umbrage at the characterization of his neighbors and community as callous, telling a reporter, "No one wants to give the people that lived here any credit. They just want to use it as a sociology lesson" ("The Night That 38 Stood By as a Life Was Lost" 1984). Forty years later, Michael would reiterate his father's position in a Letter to the Editor: "They haven't gotten it right yet, he told me, and they probably never will" (Titowsky 2004). Bernard Titowsky's long-standing unease with the media horror show that portrayed Kew Gardens and its residents so grotesquely is a testament to his place in and commitment to this local community.

When the lease on the stores expired in 1984 Titowsky moved the business again, this time to 104–29 Jamaica Avenue, below the elevated 104th Street station of the J and the Z subway lines in Richmond Hill (Titowsky, "The Austin Book Shop—Part 2"). It was there that he acquired an extensive collection of baseball books, eventually selling some to Commissioner of Major League Baseball A. Bartlett Giamatti and to the Los Angeles Dodgers, among many other clients. After Titowsky's death in 1993, Ray Harley, a patron who frequented the weekend gatherings at the bookstore, became the new owner and continues to run it today (Berry 2015).

Titowsky's daughter, Barbara Krysko, who worked in her father's bookshop, distinctly remembers that he was excited by the cache of photographs that would eventually be donated to the Calandra Institute, joyfully spreading them out on the family dining room table. Titowsky sold individual items from this original collection, and after his death the children found the remaining photos scattered in the attic of their father's Queens house. They placed them in an American Tourister suitcase—one that Bernard and Rita had used for many a vacation—and stored them for years in a closet in Michael's apartment. In 1999, Michael Titowsky contacted the late Philip V. Cannistraro, the Distinguished Professor of Italian American Studies at Queens College and curator of the exhibition *The Italians of New York* (1999–2000) at the New-York Historical Society, offering the collection to the Calandra Institute.

The Calandra Institute's Titowsky Collection contains 222 items, which in addition to photographs include two postcards, two photo albums of pasta factories, and five maps. We have categorized the collection into two sets: 69 photographs of New York City public schools from the early twentieth century and 153 items pertaining to Italian Americans. Many of them are in brittle condition; all of them require careful handling.

The New York public-school images are for the most part the same size (9³/8 x 7³/8 inches) and are printed without a border. A few of them have captions, including what appears to be a catalog number, printed in white on the image (e.g., "Exibition [sic] of Domestic Sience [sic]/ Bread Making, Theory & Practice/May 24th 1906/7321") or handwritten in pencil on the back

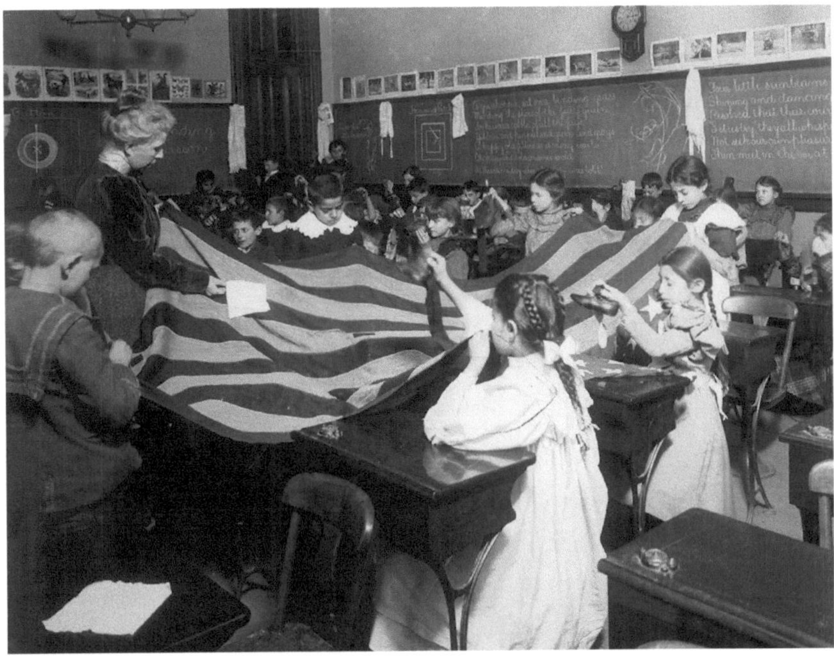

"Sewing."

("Ungraded children/motor-test"). The inscriptions inform us that the photos show public schools 37, 110, 159, and 183, as well as Stuyvesant High School in Manhattan, 140 in Brooklyn, and an unidentified playground in Corona, Queens. The dated images are from 1901, 1906, and 1910; in them, one finds depictions of a wide range of activities related to public education of the era, including girls' cooking and sewing classes, boys' shop classes, children being tested for their senses of hearing and smell, dancing (e.g., "folk dance"), and "exercising" and playing an assortment of games (e.g., bowling, volleyball). Three photos document a reenactment of the first Thanksgiving, while another three show an exhibition of "handiwork" at P.S. 166 in Manhattan from April 29, 1910.

Meanwhile, the Italian-American photographs demonstrate a panoply of immigrant lives, with group shots of mutual-aid societies, Catholic churches, and public and parochial schools. This material contains a remarkable geographic range. In addition to items from Northeast cities like Boston, Baltimore, New York City, Philadelphia, and Pittsburgh, there are also photographs from San Francisco and New Orleans. (Surprisingly, there is not a single item from Chicago.) One of the exciting aspects of the collection is the representation of Italian immigrant life in cities and towns not often associated with Italian immigration, like Alderson,

Oklahoma; Bessemer, Alabama; Laredo, Texas; Omaha, Nebraska; and Savannah, Georgia. One image (Fig. 34) comes from the border city of Ciudad Juárez, Mexico, while another is from Montreal (Fig. 11). It is not clear if the two images of empty classrooms simply labeled "Cairo" are from the United States or more conceivably, given the items seen in the school (e.g., hanging portraits of King Victor Emmanuel III and Queen Elena; an Italian-language calendar with an advertisement from a Milan company), from Egypt.

The occupations and businesses depicted vary as well. The collection shows manual laborers, both proletarians (e.g., sandhogs working underground on the Pennsylvania Railroad Station in New York City) and artisans (e.g., finishers at the Roman Bronze Works). A good number of photographs depict white-collar professionals, either Italian-language newspaper editors (Fig. 18) or presidents of immigrant-owned banks (Fig. 16), often indicated by their surrogate, the empty office. Italian-American-owned factories (Fig. 30) and other businesses are represented in abundance. The works of architects and builders such as a Greek Orthodox church in Youngstown, Ohio, built by L[uigi] Adovasio and Son Contractors, and the Terminal Station in Birmingham, Alabama, identified simply as a "costruzione italiana" (Italian construction) are also featured in the collection.

Rosangela and I selected images for the exhibition and catalog based, in part, on the diversity of location and occupations of the Italians depicted. Images like the home in Laredo (Fig. 35) or the bank in Denver (Fig. 37) are noteworthy not so much for composition or aesthetic elements but more as social documents of Italian immigrant life, and so we included such photographs. In a similar vein are the group shots of workers, voluntary association members, and schoolchildren. Also of social interest is the presence of African Americans in a few photographs, from the two clients in the Banca Popolare Fugazi (Fig. 14) to the women factory workers at the Planters Nut and Chocolate Factory (Fig. 29), for what they can potentially tell us about the relationships between Italian immigrants and African Americans. Our research informs us that in Bessemer, Alabama (Fig. 13), during the first two decades of the twentieth century, Italian-owned grocery stores catered to African-American residents. But our curating of "Reframing Italian America" also involved aesthetic considerations. The six beautiful young men in sleeveless T-shirts holding circular sheets of felt in a photographer's studio is a particularly arresting image. We were struck by the semi-abstract linear patterning of the pasta drying room (Fig. 30), with its sheets of cut vertical spaghetti and the crossed blades of the two huge fans. And then there are all those shots of empty rooms—a kitchen, an office, a classroom—deChirico-like images haunted by the ghosts of people not present.

Within the collection are a number of photographers and photography studios who are known regionally or for specializing in specific genres. The Wurts Brothers of New York City (Fig. 15), [Leon] Dadmun of Boston (Fig. 25), and the Rice Studio of Montreal (Fig. 11) are recognized by photography historians. The That Man Stone Co. out of Oklahoma City (Fig. 24) was known for panoramic photography while R[obert W.] Tebbs (Fig. 28) specialized in architectural photographs, especially church interiors. There are a few Italian immigrant photographers in the collection—A. Bellino from the Philadelphia area (Fig. 32) and D. Pace from Birmingham (Figs. 2 and 13)—but we have been unable to uncover any information about them. Frank De Maria of New York City is listed with two different New York City addresses (Figs. 9 and 39).

What we know about the people and places seen in the photographs comes from "the mouth of the text" (Sontag 1977, 108), that is, the descriptions written on the front and/or back of the mute images (Figs. 7 and 25). The textual information on the front is often rendered in a floral cursive lettering. Rosangela has engaged with the images and texts through exhaustive online research, often following up with regional historians, librarians, and archivists. In this way we have come to know some of the people and places depicted in the collection. For example, the simple street shot of buildings in Denver (Fig. 37) gives no clues to the fate of banker Prospero Frazzini who, once esteemed as a member of the immigrant elite, would die in prison after pleading guilty to embezzlement and grand larceny. The photo of Guido Podrecca, former Socialist turned Fascist government official, in a Pennsylvania pasta factory appears to be taken a short time before he died in upstate New York in 1923. We now know that the rows of children in Fig. 26 are posed in front of St. Peter's Roman Catholic Church in Pittsburgh, dedicated in 1918 and demolished in 1960 as part of slum clearance. Perhaps Rosangela's greatest achievement in investigating the images is locating the exact locations where photographs were made some hundred years ago by reading the signs hanging from buildings, cross-referencing with city directories, and then lining up the photos with Google Street Views.

The captions, coupled with the fact that a good number of the Italian-American images are mounted on heavy gray paperboard, suggest that the photographs were originally part of a previous exhibition. A revealing detail are the labels adhered to the backs of the mounted photographs, e.g., "Sala: VII/Serie: Stati Uniti America/No. 136/Parete: D" (Room: VII:/Series: United States [of] America/No. 136: Wall: D). Is it possible that the mounted images were those created and/or collected for the "Italiani all'Estero" (Italians Abroad) expositions sponsored by the Italian government from 1892 to 1911 in cities like Genoa (1892), Turin (1898; 1908),

The back of Fig. 6 with inscription and label.

Milan (1906), and Rome (1908; 1911) (Choate, 120, 186)? If so, what was the route of these objects' return to the United States? There are no definitive answers to such questions, and I can only suggest some possibilities as to the history of this somewhat mysterious collection.

Historian Mark Choate writes that national pavilions, fairs, and congresses were not only a means for Italian politicians and businessmen to rationalize the emigration of millions of Italians after the formation of the nation state in 1861 but also a way to trace, establish, and capitalize on the "capillary network" of an "emigrant nation" in terms that were understood and practiced as "colonial expansion" throughout the world (2008, 1–20; see also Audenino 2008, 111–124). Immigrant remittances and the new potential markets abroad (Cinotto 2013, 155–179) were economic benefits that encouraged Italian officials and capitalists to strengthen the emotional ties between *la madre patria* and the immigrant *colonie* (colonies) and so to foment a transnational notion of *italianità* (Choate 2008, 1–3). The "Italiani all'Estero" congresses were a means by which Italians could explain to themselves the hemorrhaging of citizens by the millions.

The oversized book *Gli italiani negli Stati Uniti d'America*, published for the 1906 Milan show, is a curious document that provides some clues to the possible connection between the

Italian expositions and the Titowsky Collection. In a section describing the charitable works of the Italian Benevolent Institute in Manhattan we find on page 308 the same exact photograph of the organization's refectory (Fig. 33) from the Titowsky Collection. While there is no other one-to-one duplication between the collection and the book, a number of overlaps and cross-references exist. The published biographies of two immigrant-owned businesses, Prospero Frazzini & Bros. Italian-American Bank of Denver and the Roman Bronze Works of Brooklyn, provide pertinent information about photographs of those companies in the collection. *Gli italiani negli Stati Uniti d'America* also has a description of the immigrant community in Sunnyside, Arkansas—the same Italian settlement where we find the photo of children standing in front of the rural schoolhouse (Fig. 6). Perhaps the most striking similarities between the two sources are the subject matter and the photographic style. Banks, factories, stores, offices, churches, schools, and farmland are shown with and without people; when present, almost all the human figures pose formally for the camera, in both the collection and the book. Similar images are used in the latter as illustrations for the 183 pages of detailed essays—what Robert Viscusi dubs "Homeric catalogs" (2013, 35)—by immigrant journalists, lawyers, priests, doctors, university professors, and others documenting the sanitary conditions, trade unions, press, and other social areas of immigrant life in the United States. If the photographs were not used specifically for the 1906 exposition (because, of course, a number of them are dated after 1906) then clearly they found a place in a comparable display.

These featured individuals and the collective they create in group shots are of an industrious, orderly, church-going, and socially engaged people. These are markedly different depictions of Italian immigrants than we find taken by others of the era such as social reformer Jacob Riis, whose muckraking work on New York City's improvised Italian slums oscillates between the "exoticizing distance" of the picturesque and the "stark racially othering" of the destitute (Bertellini 2010, 154, 158; see also Cosco 2003, 21–60; Verdicchio 2011, 115–129). A good number of the people seen in these images chose to be photographed, and thus the photos were attempts at self-representation (Ortoleva 1991, 122–123). Whether it is the Philadelphia hatmakers who set off to the photographer's studio or the scores of voluntary association members in Youngstown who posed for the panoramic image, these individuals decided to be photographed in ways of their own design. They desired to be remembered. They composed themselves before the camera, making "art of themselves" to stand "beyond time, outside of the moment, liberated from the world" (Glassie 1989, 170). These are portraits of embodied *bella figura*, the prized Italian art of creating and maintaining a good public persona through an adherence to proper comportment and the aesthetic dimensions of such a performance (see Nardini 1999). Even those who were not in complete control of the photographic enterprise—the factory workers who stopped their daily routine (Fig. 17), and the all-too-often sad-faced children lined up in front of schools—pose in the knowledge that this is a special occasion. Perhaps the most glaring exception in this regard from the images we have chosen is that of the African-American women who have not been given the opportunity to halt their factory work and to face the camera in ways of their own choosing.

The display event that was the Italian exposition was not a monolog but instead a transnational conversation between elites in Italy and the growing diaspora. As Robert Viscusi observed it was the *prominenti*, that is, the self-appointed leaders of the immigrant communities and ethnic brokers in the various host countries, who served to some degree as curators of these showcases. Writing about *Gli italiani negli Stati Uniti d'America*, Viscusi notes the book's proclamation that it was the *prominenti* in the United States who subsidized publications in exchange for profiles of themselves and their businesses that comprised "a dossier of the petit-bourgeois reality" (Viscusi 2013, 32). Viscusi goes on:

> Good manners, even to excess, provide the overwhelming tone of the second half of the book. The *prominenti* who advertise themselves here clearly want to be regarded as the equals of the people who are going to be looking at their photographs in Milan. (Ibid., 36)

The pomposity and self-aggrandizement of the *prominenti* were routinely critiqued at the time from within the community. Writing about the 1908 exposition in Turin, diplomat Luigi Villari derided the *prominenti*'s privileged position:

The idea is to bring Italy the "prominent leader" from the Italian colonies in America to obtain their views on the best way to protect emigrants. Precisely these "prominent leaders" are the ones who live by exploiting and swindling the newcomers! The "prominent leaders" of these colonies, instead of being asked their opinion and "enlightened guidance," should be put in jail or hanged. (in Choate 2008, 126) [2]

Thus the photographic enterprise that constitutes the work found in the Titowsky Collection and its (written and displayed) exposition doppelgangers warrant scrutiny from intra-ethnic and class perspectives that take into consideration hegemonic and dominant points of view concerning the formation of Italian immigrants' sense of self and community, as well as future Italian-American identities (see Saverino 2011, 153–169). These tensions within the Italian immigrant community surrounding representation—who speaks for the group at large—were part of the transnational diasporic project of nation-building that the Italian expositions fostered.

The reframing of images from the Calandra Institute's Titowsky Collection is an opportunity to discover, interpret, and enjoy these fragile and obscure visual documents. As we confront and scrutinize the silent and long-gone figures, many of them anonymous to history, and attempt to make sense of their lives and works, we are offered an opportunity to glimpse their making of both Italy and America.

Endnotes

1. None of the images in the Titowsky Collection are found in the 2001 publication *Italians Abroad: 140 Years of Photography of the Italian Communities*, edited by Michele Rak.

2. Choate only provides an English translation of this archival letter. See Cannistraro 2005, 76–86 and Saverino 2011, 153–169 for scholarly analysis of the historical *prominenti*.

Works Cited

Aldrovandi, Luigi, ed. 1906. *Gli italiani negli Stati Uniti d'America*. New York: Italian American Directory Co.

Anderson, Benedict. 1991. *Imagined Communities: Reflections on the Origin and Spread of Nationalism*. New York: Verso.

Audenino, Patrizia. 2008. "La Mosta degli italiani all'estero: prove di nazionalismo." *In Milano e l'Esposizione internazionale del 1906: La rappresentazione della modernità*, edited by Patrizia Audenino, Maria Luisa Betri, Ada Gigli Marchetti, and Carlo G. Lacaita, 111–124. Milan: FrancoAngeli.

Berry, Jess. 2015. "Top 5 Queens Independent Bookstores." http://itsqueens.com/?p=707. Accessed January 28.

Bertellini, Giorgio. 2010. *Italy in Early American Cinema: Race, Landscape, and the Picturesque*. Bloomington: Indiana University Press.

Cannistraro, Philip V. 2005. "The Duce and the Prominenti: Fascism and the Crisis of Italian of Italian American Leadership" in*Altreitalie* 31, July–December: 76–86.

Choate, Mark L. 2008. *Emigrant Nation: The Making of Italy Abroad*. Cambridge: Harvard University Press.

Cinotto, Simone. 2013. *The Italian American Table: Food, Family, and Community in New York City*. (Urbana: University of Illinois Press.

Cosco, Joseph D. 2003. *Imagining Italians: The Clash of Romance and Race in American Perceptions, 1880–1910*. Albany: State University of New York Press.

Glassie, Henry. 1989. *The Spirit of Folk Art: The Girard Collection at the Museum of International Folk Art*. New York: Harry N. Abrams.

Gansberg, Martin. 1964. "37 Who Saw Murder Didn't Call Police." *New York Times*, March 27. http://www.nytimes.com/1964/03/27/37-who-saw-murder-didnt-call-the-police.html?_r=0. Accessed February 4, 2015.

Kaufman, Leslie. 2013. "Timeless Book May Require Some Timely Fact Checking." In *New York Times*. http://www.nytimes.com/2013/01/31/books/releasing-old-nonfiction-books-when-facts-have-changed.html?pagewanted=all. January 31. Accessed January 30, 2015.

Lemann, Nicholas. 2014. "A Call for Help." *The New Yorker*, March 10. http://www.newyorker.com/magazine/2014/03/10/a-call-for-help. Accessed January 28, 2015.

Nardini, Gloria. 1999. *Che Bella Figura! The Power of Performance in an Italian Ladies' Club in Chicago*. Albany: SUNY Press.

"The Night That 38 Stood by as a Life was Lost." 1984. *New York Times*, March 12. http://www.nytimes.com/1984/03/12/nyregion/the-night-that-38-stood-by-as-a-life-was-lost.html. Accessed January 28, 2015.

Ortoleva, Peppino. 1991. "Una fonte difficile: La fotografia e la storia dell'emigrazione." in *Altreitalie* 5, April: 120–131.

Rak, Michele. 2001. *Gli italiani all'estero: 140 anni di fotografie delle comunità italiane/ Italians Abroad: 140 Years of Photography of the Italian Communities*. Rome: BCM.

Rasenberger, Jim. 2004. "Kitty, 40 Years Later," *New York Times*, February 8. http://www.nytimes.com/2004/02/08/nyregion/kitty-40-years-later.html?pagewanted=all. Accessed January 30, 2015.

Saverino, Joan. 2011. "Italians in Public Memory: Pageantry, Power, and Imagining the 'Italian American' in Reading, Pennsylvania." In *Italian Folk: Vernacular Culture in Italian-American Lives,* edited by Joseph Sciorra, 153–169. New York: Fordham University Press.

Sciorra, Joseph. 2015. *Built with Faith: Italian American Imagination and Catholic Material Culture in New York*. Knoxville: University of Tennessee Press.

Sontag, Susan. 1977. *On Photography*. New York: Dell Publishing Company, Inc.

Titowsky, Bernard. 1964. *American History: A Guide to Student Reading for Teachers and Librarians*. Brookhaven, N.J.: McKinley Publishing Co.

Titowsky, Michael. "The Austin Book Shop—Part 1." http://www.oldkewgardens.com/ss-lefferts-1015.html. Accessed January 28, 2015.

Titowsky, Michael. "The Austin Book Shop—Part 2." http://www.oldkewgardens.com/ss-lefferts-1015-1.html. Accessed January 28, 2015.

Titowsky, Michael B. 2014. "From Tragedy, A Sense of Community" [Letter to the Editor]. *New York Times*, February 15. http://www.nytimes.com/2004/02/15/nyregion/l-from-tragedy-a-sense-of-community-395498.html. Accessed January 28, 2015.

Verdicchio, Pasquale. 2011. *Looters, Photographers, and Thieves: Aspects of Italian Photographic Culture in the Nineteenth and Twentieth Centuries*. N.J.: Fairleigh Dickinson University Press.

Viscusi, Robert. 2013. "The Universal Exposition." In *Strangers in a Strange Land: A Survey of Italian Language American Books (1830–1945)*, edited by James J. Periconi, 30–41. New York: Bordighera Press.

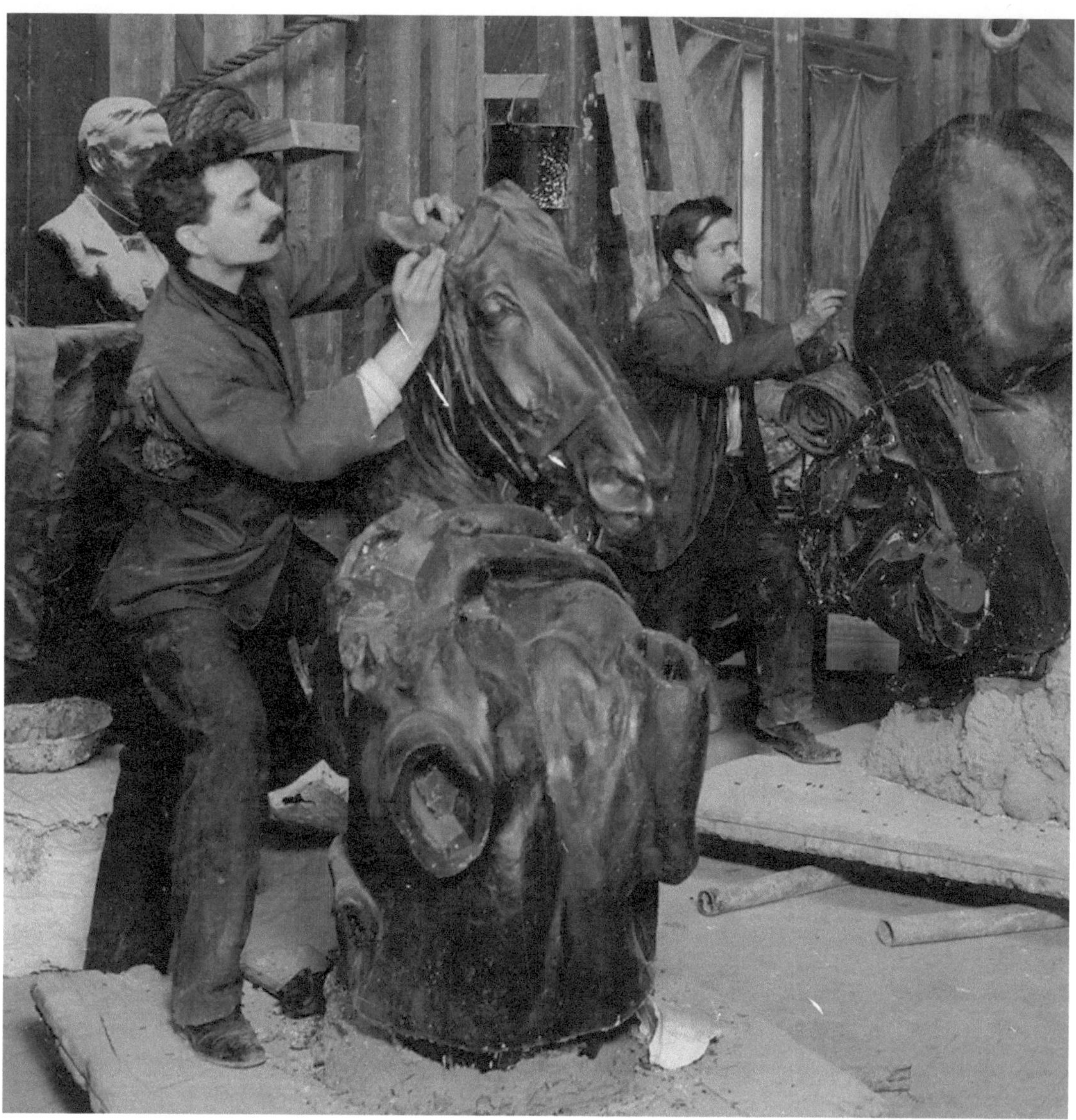

Detail: Roman Bronze Works

LENSES ONTO THE PAST

THE PHOTOGRAPHS OF THE BERNARD TITOWSKY COLLECTION

DOMINIQUE PADURANO

THE IMAGES in the Calandra Institute's Bernard Titowsky Collection paint a fascinating portrait of Italian-American life between the end of the nineteenth century and the middle of the twentieth. Photographs of workers often attest to the immigrants' artistry and strength, while others point toward the business acumen of those not pictured, the likely owners of the factory on display. Hundreds of Italian-American children at schools proclaim their parents' reason for emigrating—to secure a better life for their kids. That Italian-Americans adapted and flourished upon immigrating is evident from these images, as is a determination to maintain ties with their traditions. In these remarkable photographs, we see people inventing what it means to be both Italian and American during the early years of the last century.

Fleeing natural disasters, high taxes and rents, and scarce resources and opportunities at home, Italians were the United States' largest European immigrant group between 1880 and 1920, numbering slightly more than four million (Daniels 1990). Since the vast majority left Italy in search of better economic opportunities than they had at home, it is unsurprising that the largest group of photographs within the Titowsky Collection depicts Italian immigrants at work. A particularly striking image shows six hatmakers, all dressed in tank tops (Fig. 41). The young men, who appear to be about twenty years old, stand in front of a formal background, holding pieces of felt in various stages of becoming hats. This photograph emerges from the nineteenth-century genre of group portraits of male laborers (Sandweiss 1991). Civil War soldiers, telegraph-line layers, lumberjacks—as well as hatmakers—often posed for a studio portrait in "work clothes" (hence our hatters in their undershirts) and with coworkers and the tools of their trade. The resulting photographs memorialize the men's professional skill and their relationship to others in their labor fraternity. In "Gruppo Cappellai Italiani," these young men also joined this symbolic band of brothers and workingmen. "Gruppo Cappellai

Italiani" also testifies to the pride that so many immigrants took in their crafts. Far from the startled look of Jacob Riis's often disheveled subjects, these artisans engage the camera's lens with directness and seriousness of purpose, claiming their rightful place as American workers.

The Titowsky Collection boasts a second type of laborers' photograph. Taken on the shop floor instead of in the artist's studio, this type of photograph usually depicted many more workers than the formal portrait did. One such image (Fig. 17) adds complexity to the history of Italian workers in the United States. While seminal studies in the field have described Italian immigrants' tendency to labor as a family unit (Yans-McLaughlin 1977) or in single-sex environments (Enstad 1999, Peiss 1986), this photograph depicts adult men and women who do not appear to be family members working closely together on the same shop floor. While anecdotal, this image is not unique in the Titowsky Collection, as a photograph of the Ralph Ring Company (not pictured) shows a similar scene. It is interesting to speculate whether further investigation of such photographic evidence might alter the traditional interpretation of Italians' work customs during this period.

Two important sectors of Italian labor in the United States—the building trades and food sales and preparation—are handsomely represented in the collection. Train stations in various phases of construction (Figs. 7 and 8), completed churches (Figs. 28 and 39), a work crew (Fig. 32), and a group of artisans (Fig. 15) illustrate Italians' integral role in building and beautifying modern America. Just as Italians brought their craftsmanship in stone with them to the United States, so, too did they immigrate with their culinary prowess. Though poverty had denied meat to many in Italy, immigrants here took advantage of this country's abundance to indulge in frequent carnivory (Diner 2003). "Volpi Packing Co." (Fig. 10) shows one such venture, the inside of a salami factory in St. Louis, Missouri. In another photograph from Lebanon, Pennsylvania (Fig. 30), thousands of pieces of spaghetti hang from wooden beams while fresh fruit—another Italian staple—is sold proudly by Pietro Giammusso (Fig. 13) and other unidentified Italians (Fig. 36). Even on a large scale, Italian businesses dealt in food: Hazelnuts and chocolates were sorted and manufactured in Amedeo Obici's Suffolk, Virginia, factory (Fig. 29).

Giammusso and Obici are hardly the only business owners featured in the Titowsky Collection. Banks and bankers from Ohio to California form their own small group of photographic subjects. Calling to mind the check-cashing and money-sending services in Spanish-speaking parts of American cities today, an image of A. di Fronzo of Cleveland shows a business that changed foreign currency as well as acting as a steamship agent in 1927 (Fig. 12). Meanwhile, the well-appointed Banca Popolare Fugazi of San Francisco (Fig. 14) and Prospero Frazzini & Bros. Italian American Bank in Denver (Fig. 37)—the latter with branches in Ogden, Utah; Pocatello, Idaho; and San Pietro Avellana, Italy—demonstrated the impressive reach of early immigrants' enterprises.

Indeed, the geographical variety represented in the Titowsky Collection is perhaps one of its biggest surprises and surely one of its greatest strengths. While Italians' influence in the wine country of California might surprise few, their impact in the South, especially outside the city of New Orleans, is less well-known. These photographs attest to vibrant communities of Italians in Sunnyside, Arkansas (Fig. 6); Birmingham (Fig. 2) and Bessemer (Fig. 13), Alabama; Savannah, Georgia (Fig. 23); Alderson, Oklahoma (Fig. 24); Laredo (Fig. 35) and El Paso (Fig. 19), Texas; and even right across the El Paso border in Ciudad Juárez, Mexico (Fig. 34). Just as New Orleans's Italians and other ethnics played a role in the development of African-American jazz (Raeburn 1991), these photographs lead one to muse on how the Italian Americans of these locales interacted with others who lived there.

For example, were the young black boys standing in the center of the photograph of Pietro Giammusso's fruit store (Fig. 13) merely passing by when the photographer snapped the shutter? Or were they delivery boys, as the taller boy's basket suggests? If so, were they hired because they likely spoke English, and perhaps the boy at the extreme left—Giammuso's son?—did not? Were the two boys even a pair? Friends? Brothers? Neighbors? Or strangers? After all, one wears shoes, while the other does not. How did Giammusso treat the boys, if they did work for him (or if they just frequented his shop)? Their central placement in the photograph seems interesting, if not noteworthy. (Given that Pietro and the adult woman who might be his wife and the other children are not grouped together, for example, it's possible that the photographer took the picture in haste or that he was not in pursuit of a conventional composition.) What might the possible relationship between Giammusso, other members of his family, and the two boys imply, if anything, about the relations of other Italian immigrants to the South and their African-American neighbors?

The photograph "Import-export business of fruit and other Mexican and American products" (Fig. 36) raises similar questions about interethnic relations between Italians and Mexicans. This informal outdoor portrait features fruit packers, some of whom appear to be European and others Mexican. Did Italians and Mexicans typically work side by side in Texas and the

Southwest? Did they attend the same Catholic churches? Did the linguistic proximity of Italian and Spanish permit the two immigrant groups to labor and socialize well together? What, if any, cultural offspring were born from these relationships? Operas sung in Spanish, for example, or pizza topped with chipotle? Hybrid religious practices? A patois of Spanish and Italian, bypassing the use of English altogether? Or was this import-export affair strictly business, a product of consumers' needs being met by immigrant entrepreneurship, like the author of "Keep Warm Get a Sweater for $1.00" (Fig. 38)? While consumer demand almost certainly played a part in the genesis of the "import-export business," cultural mixing was a likely result among the Mexican, Italian, and American elements of this enterprise.

Ultimately, it is probable that this multicultural workplace functioned after the manner of schools—the collection's last major subject—as crucibles of Americanization. While religious education (Figs. 22, 26, 27, 28, and 40) undoubtedly reinforced some Italian mores, the fact that both girls and boys are pictured together in these photographs suggests the possible move toward less strict, more mainstream American behaviors on the part of some Italian immigrant families. (Nevertheless, the relative lack of older girls in pictures from the Pittsburgh, Pennsylvania [Fig. 26], school suggests that some traditional patriarchal attitudes about the value of educating daughters might have persisted in the Italian community there.) Moreover, the display of the American flag even in Catholic schools signals at least the symbolic importance these institutions placed on allegiance to one's new country. In public schools, patriotism occupied an even more prominent place—when the camera was present (Fig. 5). The diverse faces populating the Denver school in this image once again hint at the multiple avenues that "Americanization" may have taken. The profusion of American flags suggests a heavy top-down approach, whereby teachers and administrators inculcated their charges with the nation's values. Yet, the girls' faces—Italians, certainly, but daughters of Ireland and perhaps elsewhere, as well—evoke the possibility that the school's many newcomers co-created modern American culture together, from the bottom up.

In all, the workers, business owners, bankers, men, women, and children of the Titowsky Collection leave us with a rich and varied picture of Italian-American life during the years of the group's heaviest migration. Like many old and treasured photographs, the collection's greatest and most poignant value extends far beyond the images themselves, into the questions and musings these faces of the past evoke in the minds and hearts of viewers today.

Works Cited

Chinn, Sarah. 2008. *Inventing Modern Adolescence: The Children of Immigrants in Turn-of-the-Century America*. New Brunswick, NJ: Rutgers University Press.

Daniels, Roger. 1990. *Coming to America: A History of Immigration and Ethnicity in American Life*. New York: Harper Perennial.

Diner, Hasia. 2003. *Hungering for America: Italian, Irish and Jewish Foodways in the Age of Migration*. Cambridge, MA: Harvard University Press.

Enstad, Nan. 1999. *Ladies of Labor, Girls of Adventure: Working Women, Popular Culture and Labor Politics at the Turn of the Twentieth Century*. New York: Columbia University Press.

Mormino, Gary R. 2002. *Immigrants on the Hill: Italians in St. Louis, 1882–1982*. University of Missouri Press.

Peiss, Kathy. 1986. *Cheap Amusements: Working Women and Leisure in Turn-of-the-Century New York*. Philadelphia: Temple University Press

Raeburn, Bruce Boyd. 1991. "Jazz and the Italian Connection." *Jazz Archivist*, May: 1–5. http://jazz.tulane.edu/sites/all/themes/Howard_Tilton/docs/jazz_archivist/Jazz_Archivist_vol6no1_May_1991.pdf#jazz. Accessed January 3, 2014.

Sandweiss, Martha, ed. 1991. *Photography in Nineteenth-Century America*. New York: Harry N. Abrams.

Yans-McLaughlin, Virginia. 1977. *Family and Community: Italian Immigrants in Buffalo, 1880–1930*. Ithaca, NY: Cornell University Press.

Catalog

Dimensions: height precedes width.

Figure numbers with asterisks indicate items in the exhibition.

Titles in quotes are verbatim inscriptions from the front or back of the photographs.

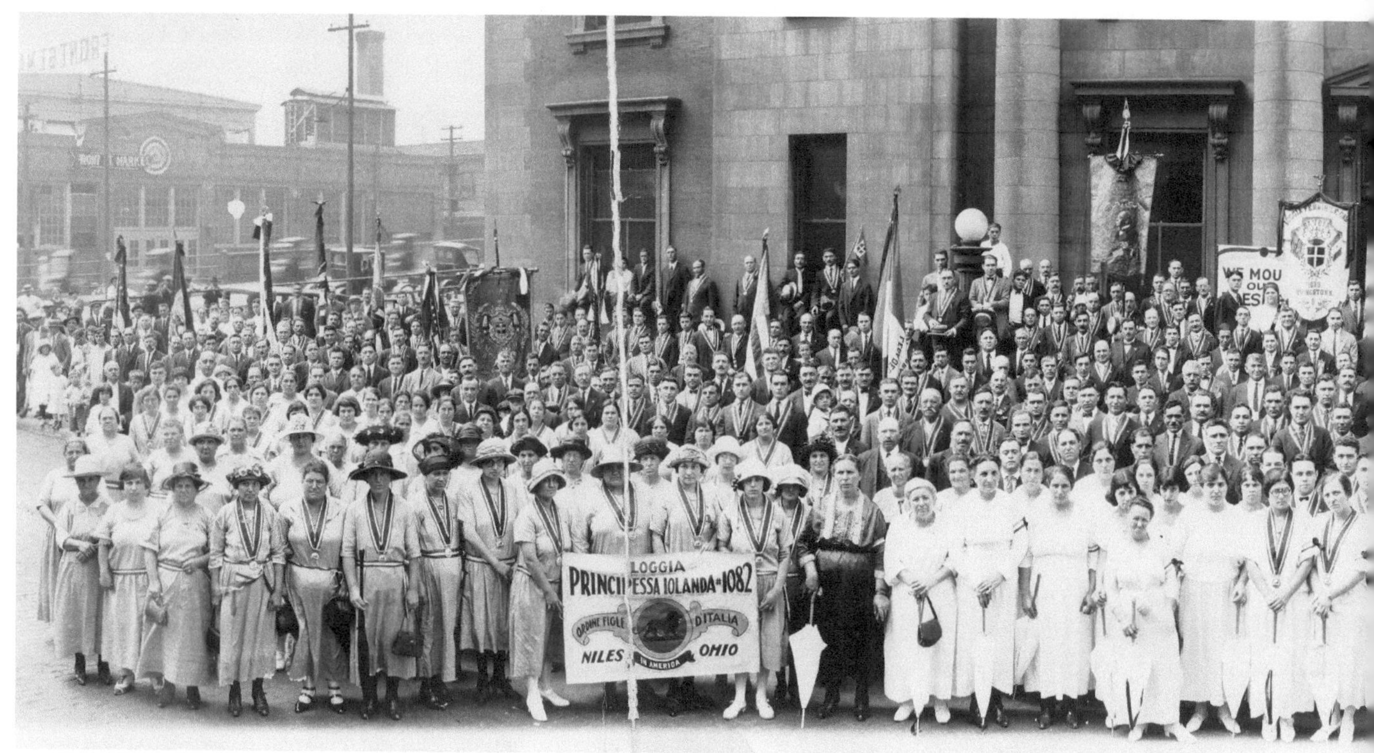

FIGURE 1*
Order Sons of Italy in America
Convention
Youngstown, Ohio
Photograph by Charles R. Brown,
Youngstown
August 4–7, 1923.
9¼ x 37 inches

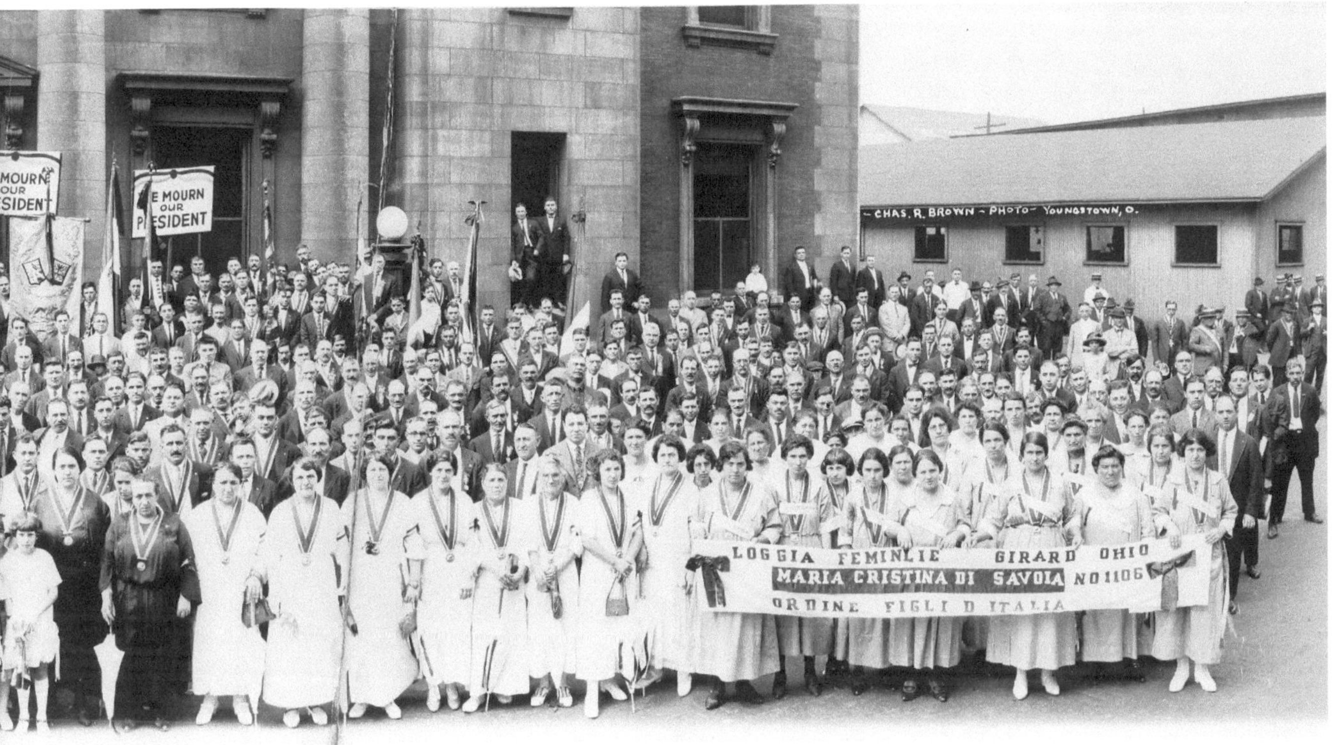

This photograph was taken at Front and Market Streets in downtown Youngstown, at the present site of the City Hall annex. The signs reading "We Mourn Our President" visible at the rear of the crowd refer to Warren G. Harding, who died on August 2, 1923.

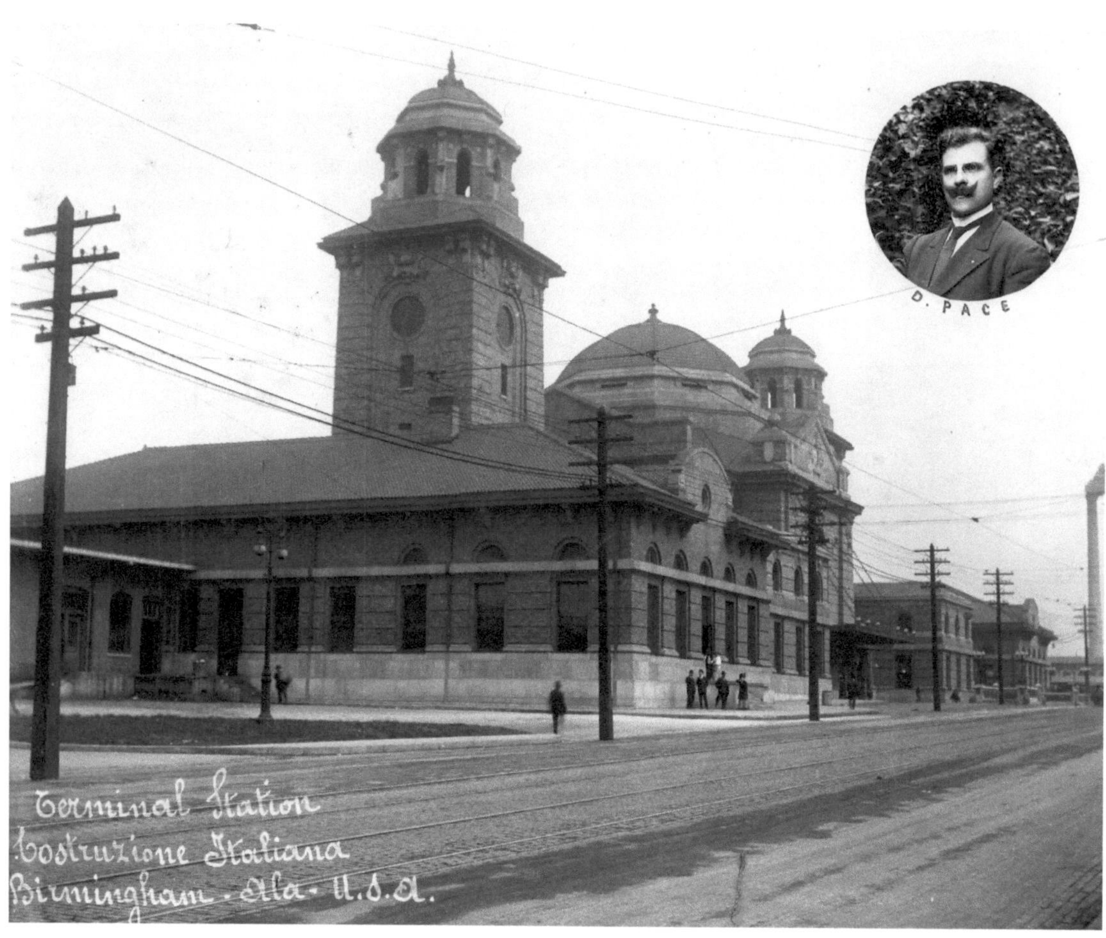

FIGURE 2
Terminal Station
"Costruzione Italiana" [Italian construction]
Birmingham, Alabama
Photograph by D. Pace, Birmingham
Date unknown
7¾ x 9⅝ inches

This is an example from the Titowsky Collection of Italian immigrant involvement in building construction. Designed by P. Thornton Marye and completed in 1909, Terminal Station was demolished in 1969 despite outcry from local preservationists. Terminal Station played a role in Civil Rights history when in 1957 African-American activists Rev. Fred Shuttlesworth and Ruby Shuttlesworth challenged the station's segregated waiting rooms.

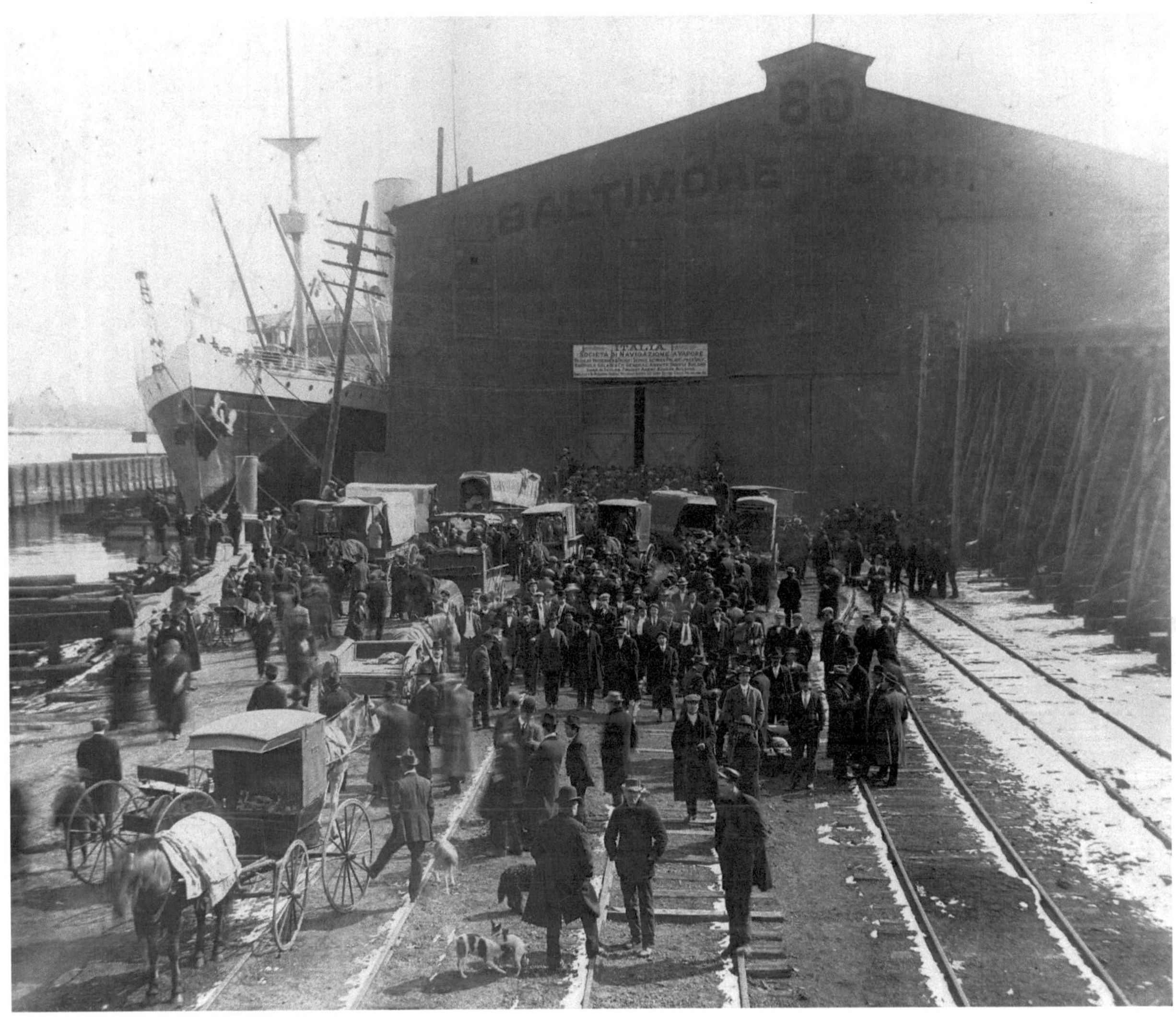

FIGURE 3
"Sbarco di emigranti Italiani"
[Disembarkation of Italian emigrants]
Philadelphia, Pennsylvania
Photographer unknown
Date unknown
10¾ x 13⅛ inches

The signage on the building indicates that this is Pier 80 on the Delaware River, which was used by the Baltimore and Ohio Railroad until it was destroyed by a fire in 1912. A smaller sign shows that the pier was also used by the Italia Società di Navigazione a Vapore to discharge its immigrant passengers. The Italia Line would later use Pier 19 at Vine Street.

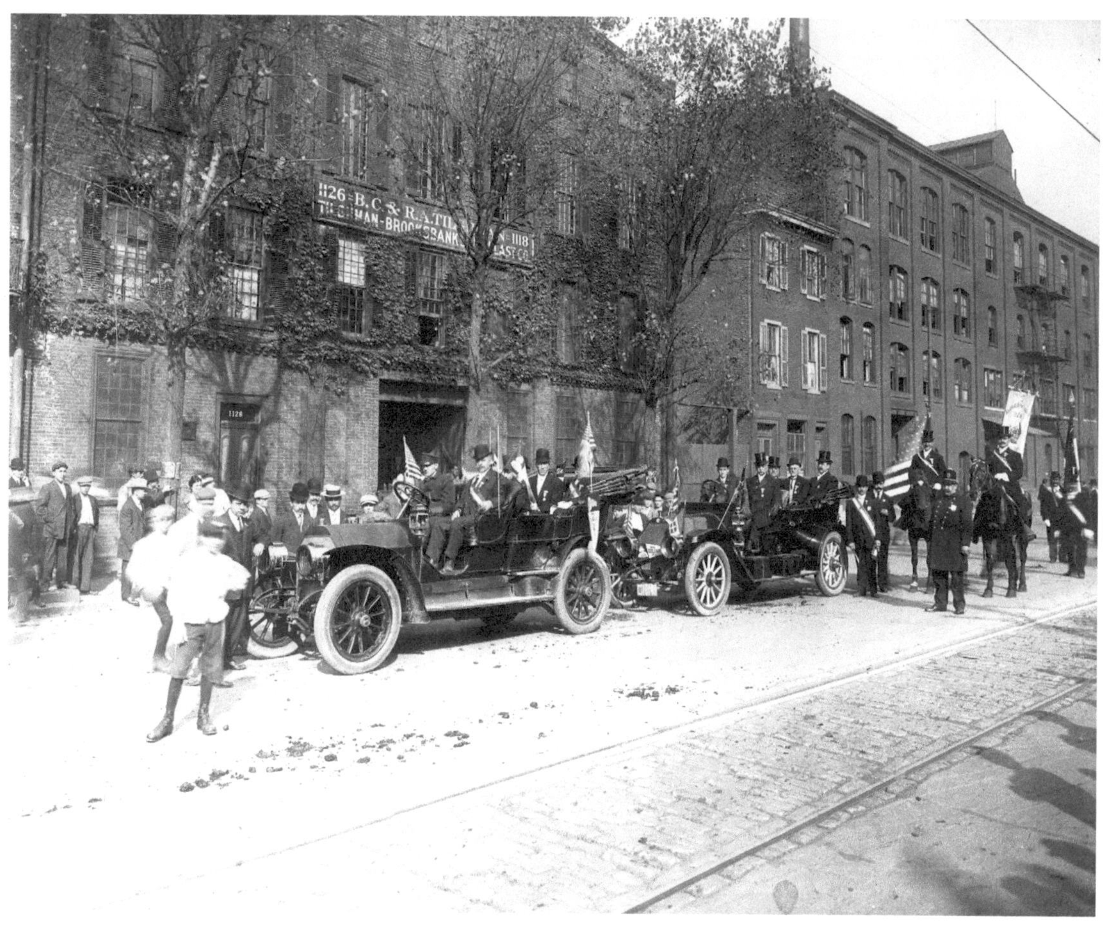

FIGURE 4*
Commemoration for Christopher Columbus
Philadelphia, Pennsylvania
Photographer unknown
Date unknown
10½ x 13½ inches

This photograph was taken in front of Tilghman-Brooksbank Sand Blast Company, 1126 South 11th Street, not far from the Italian Market on South 9th Street.

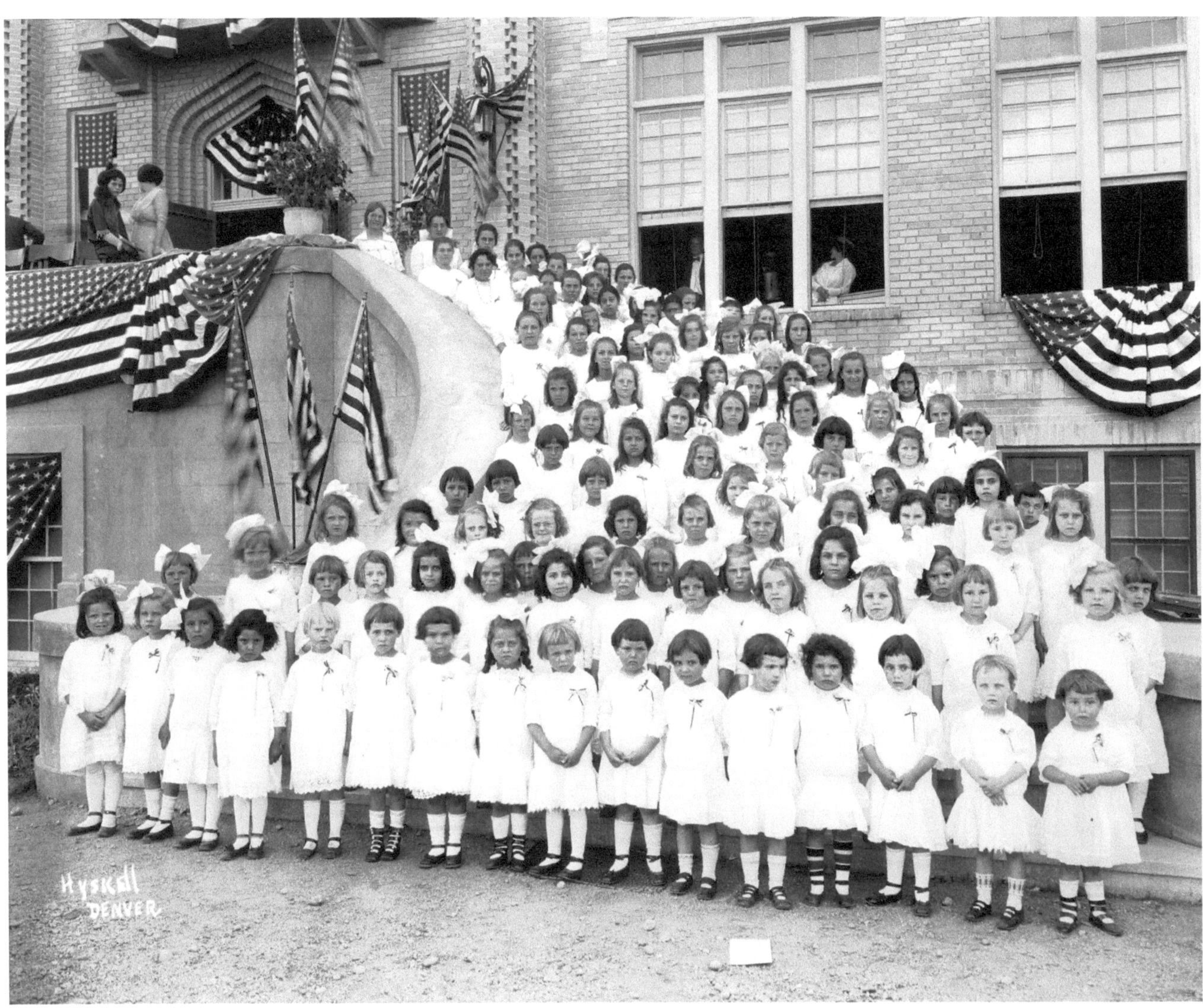

FIGURE 5*
Denver, Colorado
Photograph by Hyskell
Date unknown
$7^{1/2}$ x $9^{1/2}$ inches

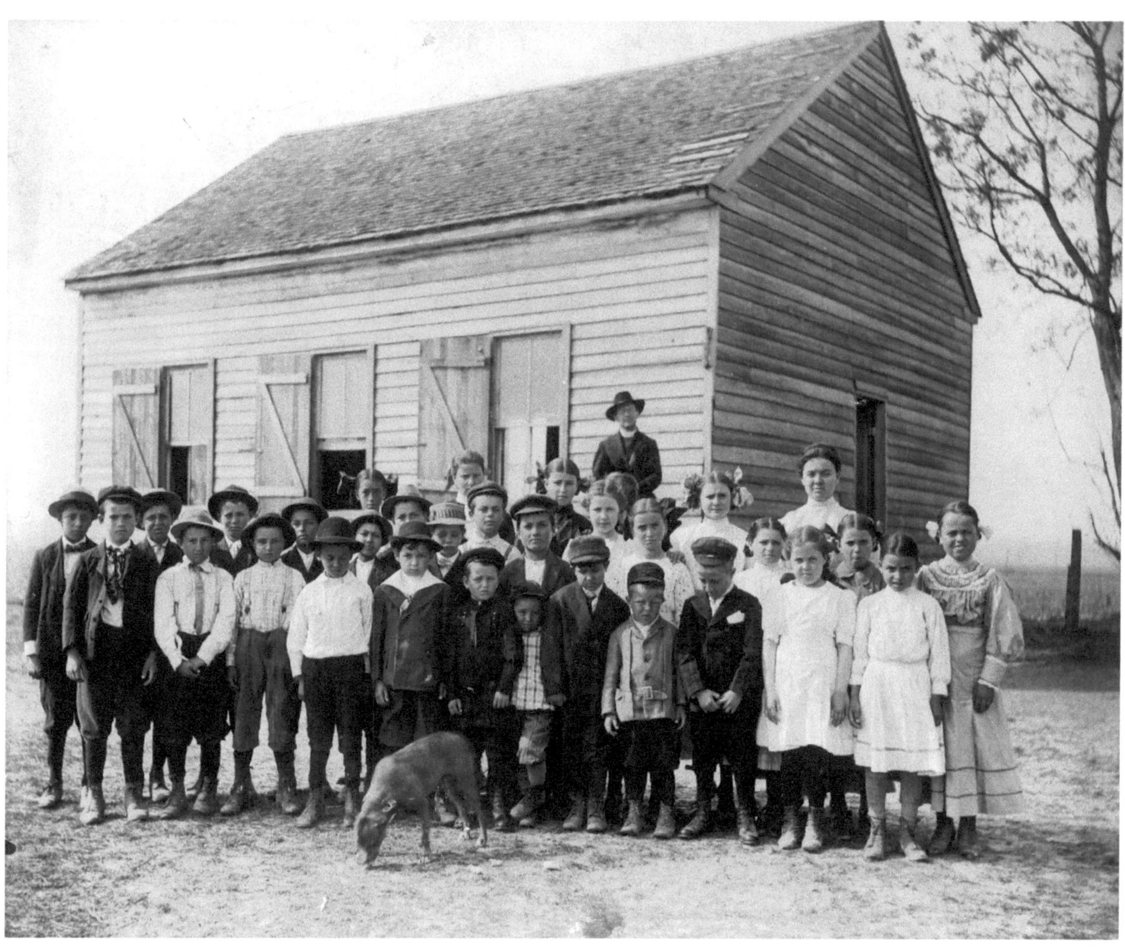

FIGURE 6*
"Colonia di (fittavoli) Sunnyside, Ark. Una delle tre scuole esistenti nella Colonia." [Colony of (tenants) Sunnyside, Ark. One of the three schools present in the Colony.]
Sunnyside, Arkansas
Photograph by Bradley
March 14, 1911
$7^{5}/_{8}$ x $9^{5}/_{8}$ inches

Sunnyside, a cotton plantation in Chicot County, Arkansas, was founded in the 1830s. The land was worked by slaves and after the Civil War by black sharecroppers. The presence of Italian Americans there dates to 1895, when Austin Corbin, then-owner of what had become a 10,000-acre property, arranged for a settlement of Italians at Sunnyside. Within a few years many of these immigrants, unsatisfied with the conditions, left for other areas of the South. For instance, Father Pietro Bandini, who may be the priest pictured in this photo, led a group to resettle in Tontitown, Arkansas. In 1907, the U.S. Justice Department began an investigation into the possible violation of labor and peonage laws in the Sunnyside system; by 1920, nearly all the Italian Americans had moved elsewhere. As indicated in the inscription on the verso, the school pictured here provided instruction to the Italian and American children of Sunnyside.

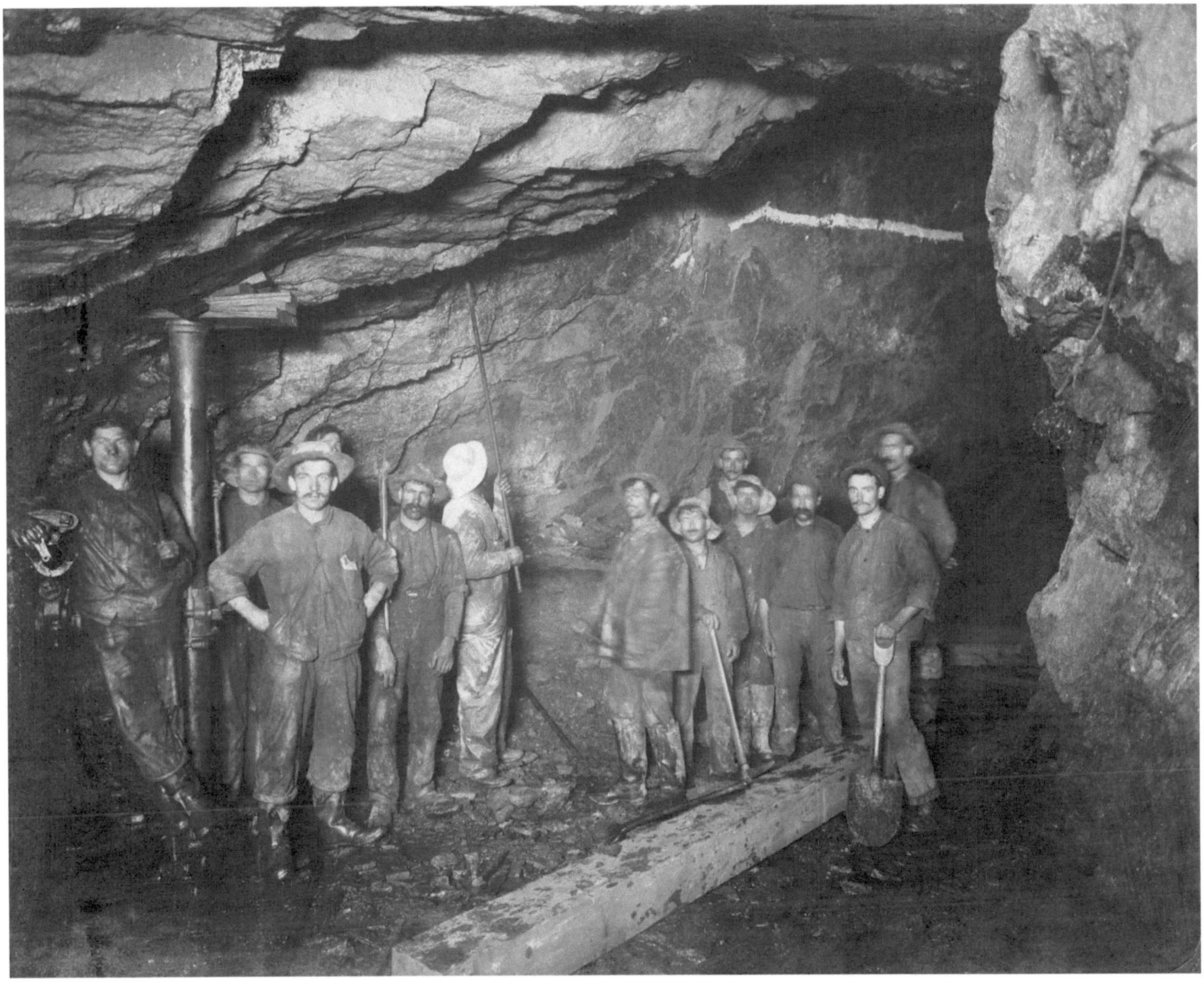

FIGURE 7*

"Gli Italiani nella costruzione della Stazione di New York della Pennsylvania R.R. Co. Lavorando nella galleria." [Italians in the construction of the Pennsylvania Railroad Company's New York station. Working in the tunnels.]
New York, New York
Photographer unknown
Date unknown
7½ x 9 inches

Right: matted photograph with labels

Based on the inscription on the verso, these workers might be engaged in the construction of the cross-town tunnels of the New York Tunnel Extension of the Pennsylvania Railroad (1905–1909), a project that led to the construction of Pennsylvania Station, which opened in 1910 and was demolished in 1963.

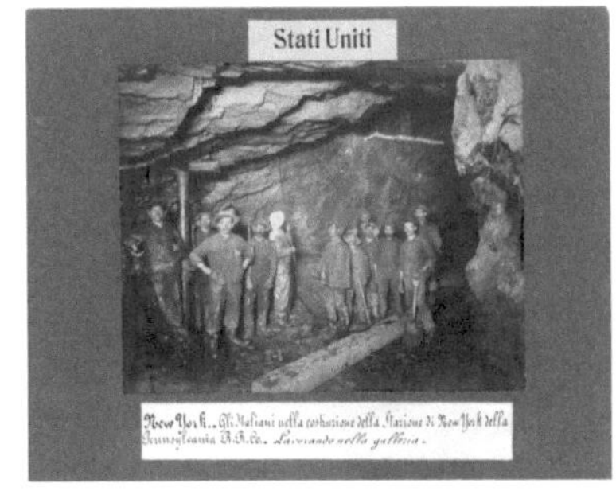

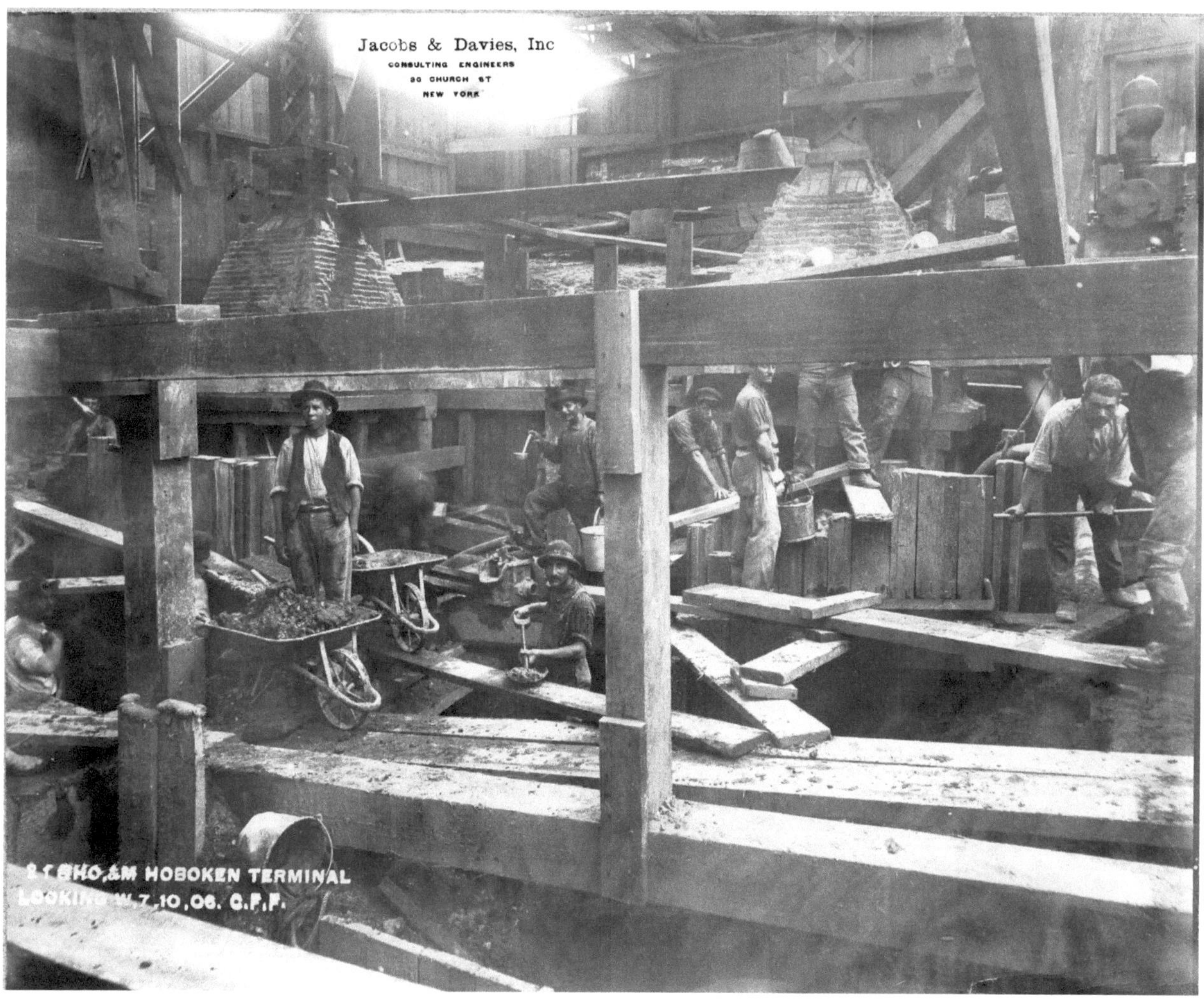

FIGURE 8

"Gli Italiani nei grandi lavori di costruzione—Tunnels. Ferrovia subacquea nel fiume Hudson, NY. I lavori di scavo per una delle stazioni" [Italians involved in large-scale construction projects—Tunnels. Underwater railway in the Hudson River, NY. Excavation work for one of the stations]
Hoboken, New Jersey
Photographer unknown
July 10, 1906
7½ x 9½ inches

This is one of six photographs mounted to a large board depicting construction of the Hudson and Manhattan Railroad tunnels and stations, now operated by the Port Authority Trans-Hudson Corporation (PATH).

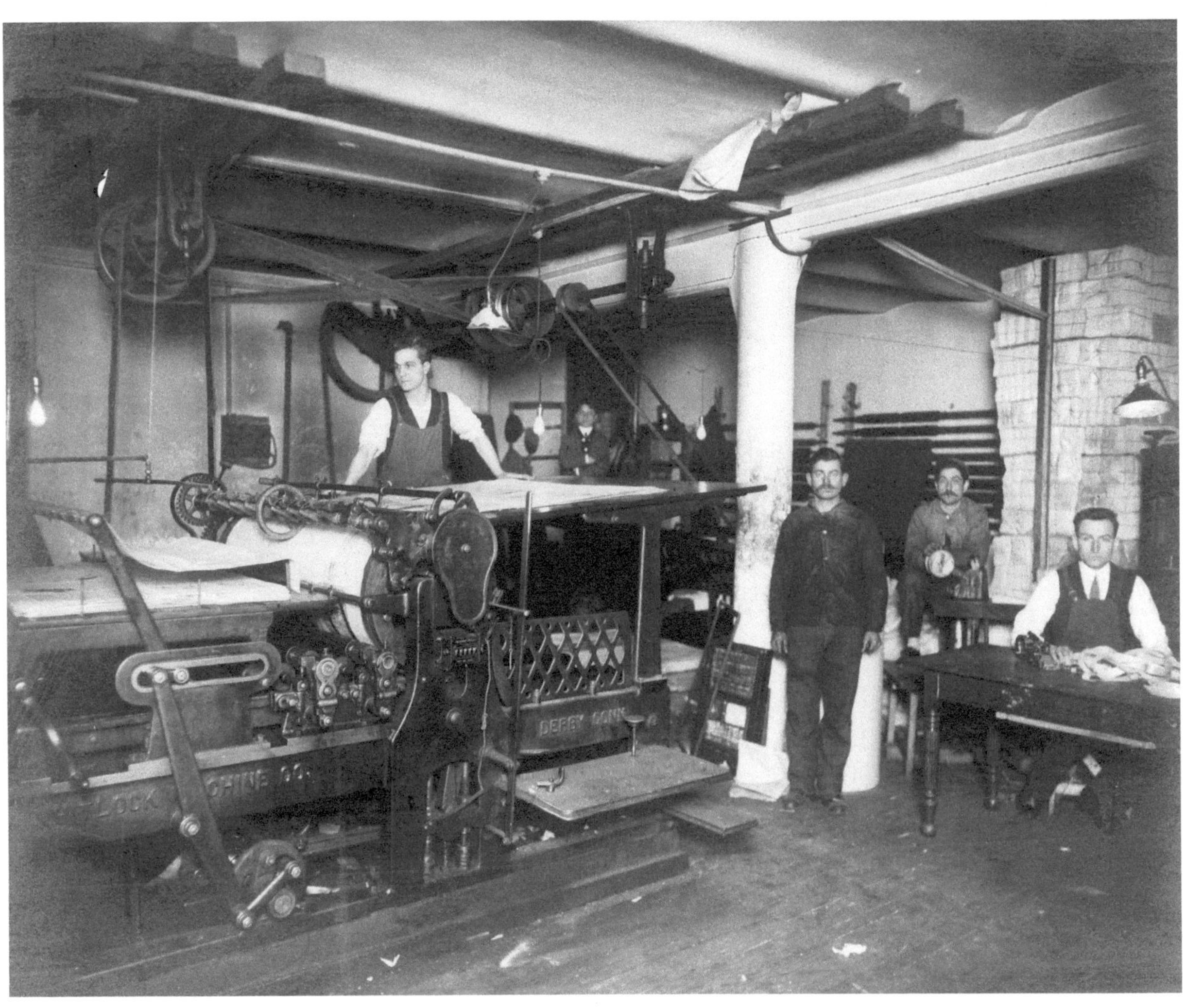

FIGURE 9*
Il Giornale Italiano
"Tipografia—Macchina 'Whitlock' per giornali settimanali" [Printing press—Whitlock Machine for weekly newspapers]
Photograph by F. De Maria, New York
Date unknown
11 x 13¾ inches

Celestino Piva and Michele Grella founded the New York-based *Il Giornale Italiano* in 1909. In 1917, its owners acquired the newspapers *L'Araldo* and *Il Telegrafo*. Edited by Ercole Cantelmo, *Il Giornale Italiano* was published until 1919.

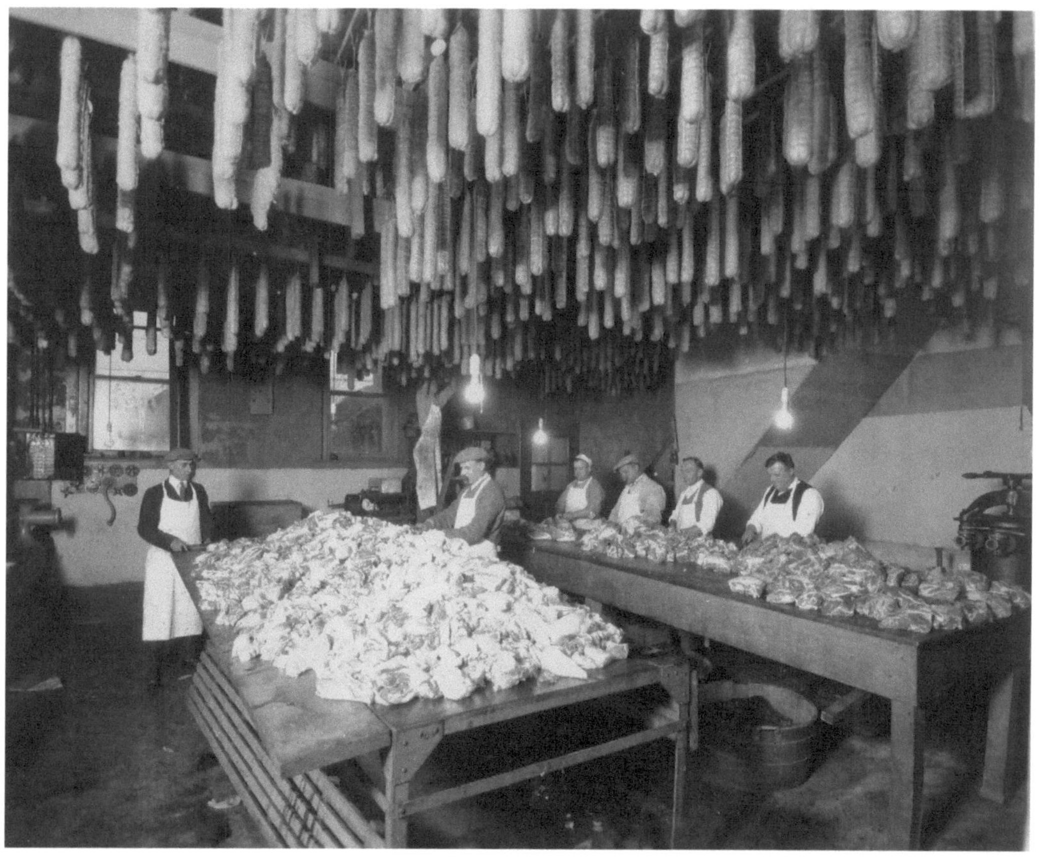

FIGURE 10*
Volpi Packing Company
"Interno di un reparto di lavorazione salumi" [Inside the section for cured meat production]
St. Louis, Missouri
Photographer unknown
Date unknown
7¼ x 9 inches

Giovanni Volpi immigrated to the United States from Milan in 1900. Two years later he started producing and selling salami locally in St. Louis with his business partner and future brother-in-law Gino Pasetti. When Volpi died in 1957, his nephew Armando—who immigrated in 1938—took over the company, and Armando's daughter Lorenza followed in his footsteps upon his retirement in 2002. Since the 1980s, Volpi Foods's products have been distributed nationally and internationally.

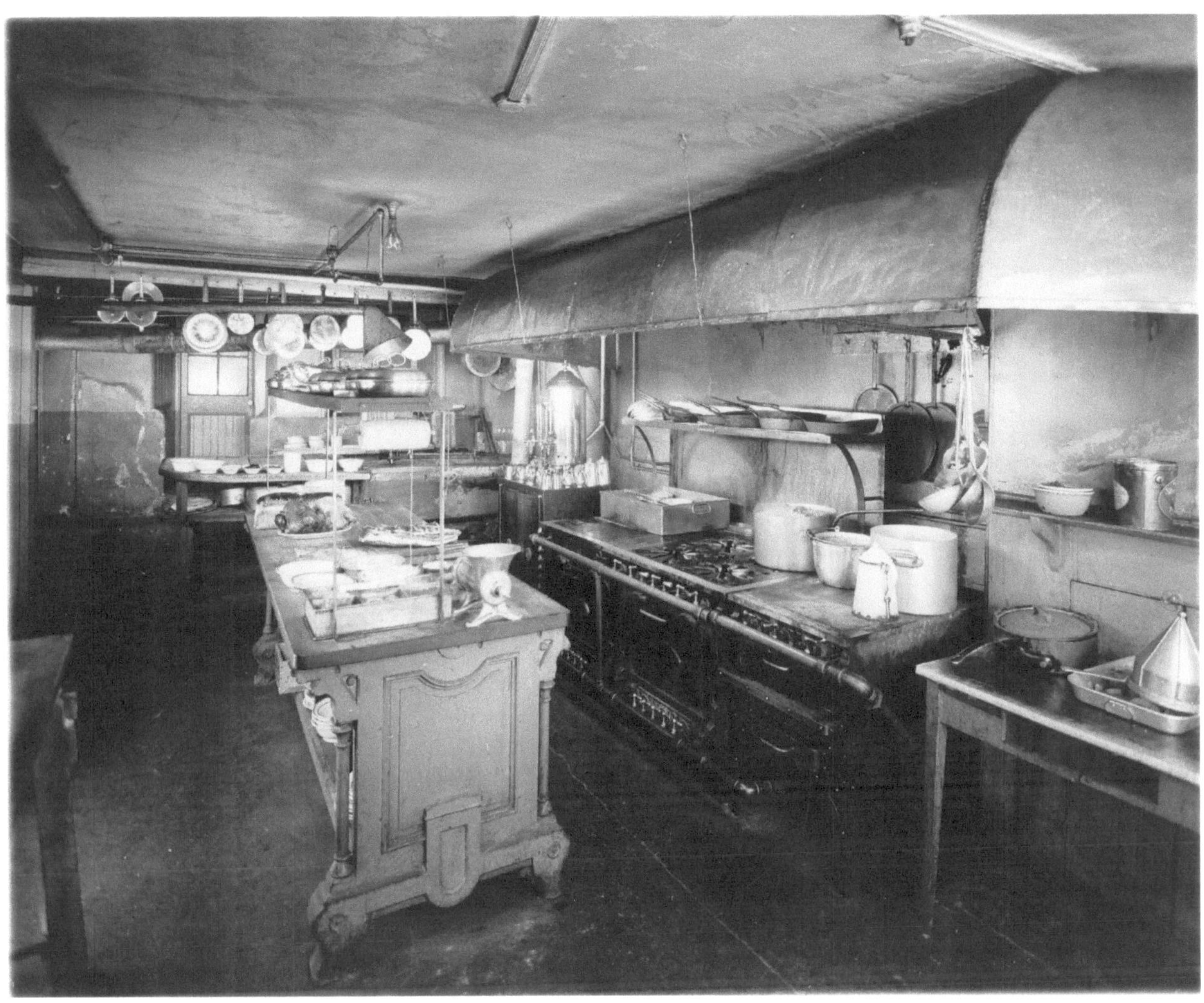

FIGURE 11
Kitchen of Roma Restaurant
Montreal, Canada
Photograph by Rice Studio Limited
Date unknown
8 x 9⅞ inches

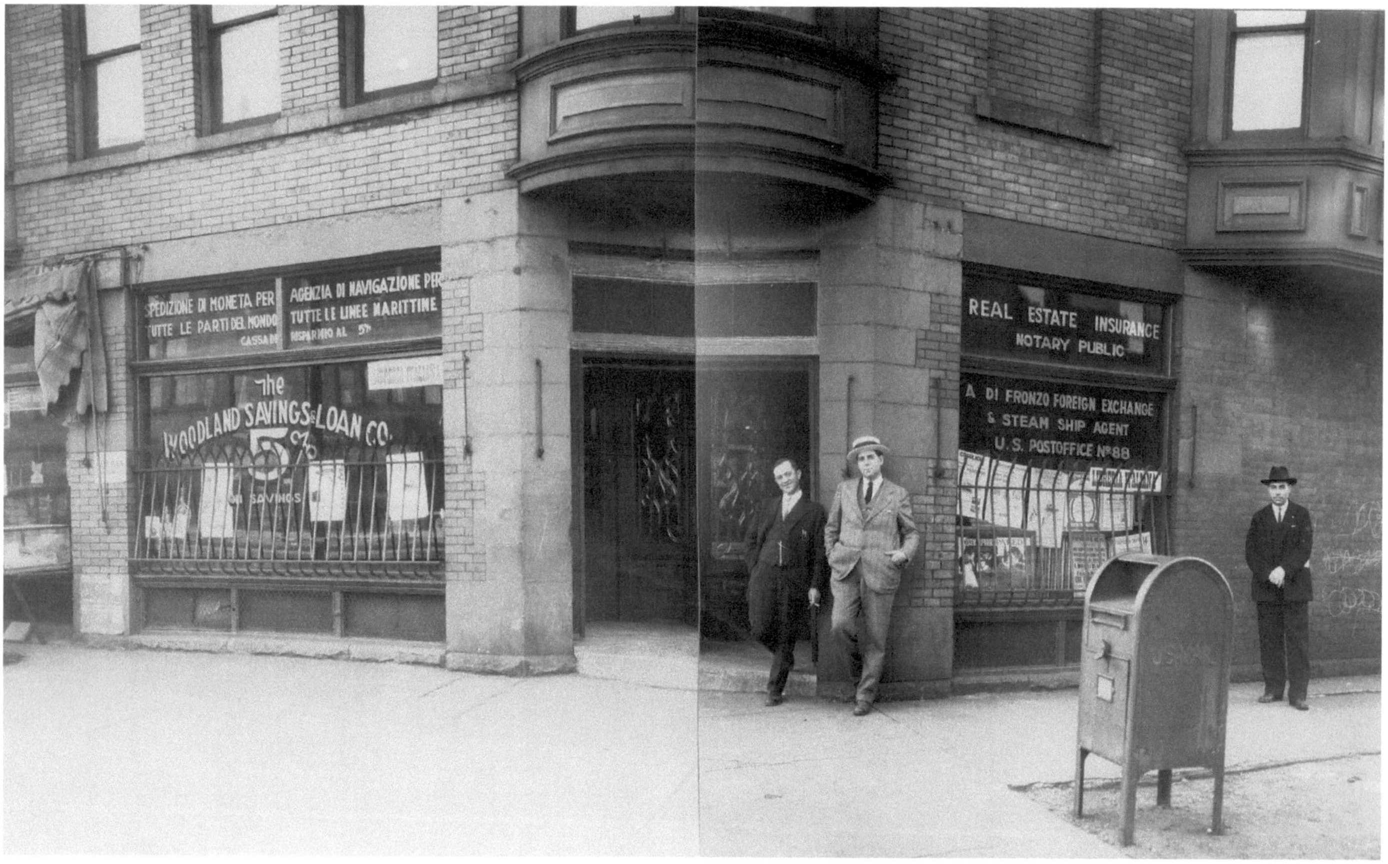

FIGURE 12*
The Woodland Savings and Loan Co.
1719 Woodland Avenue, Cleveland, Ohio
Photographer unknown
June 9, 1927
7 1/4 x 12 3/4 inches

Right: detail of back showing inscription

Antonio Di Fronzo's Woodland Savings and Loan Co. was incorporated in 1921. Woodland Avenue ran through Cleveland's first major Italian-American neighborhood, known as Big Italy. The Italian-American population began to decline in the 1930s, and much of the neighborhood was lost to urban renewal and highway construction in the 1950s.

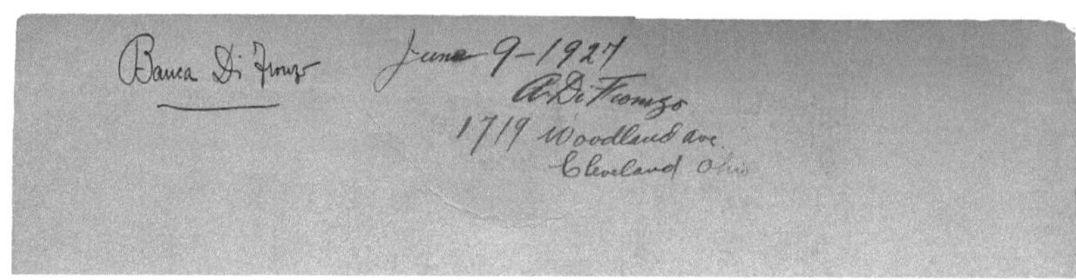

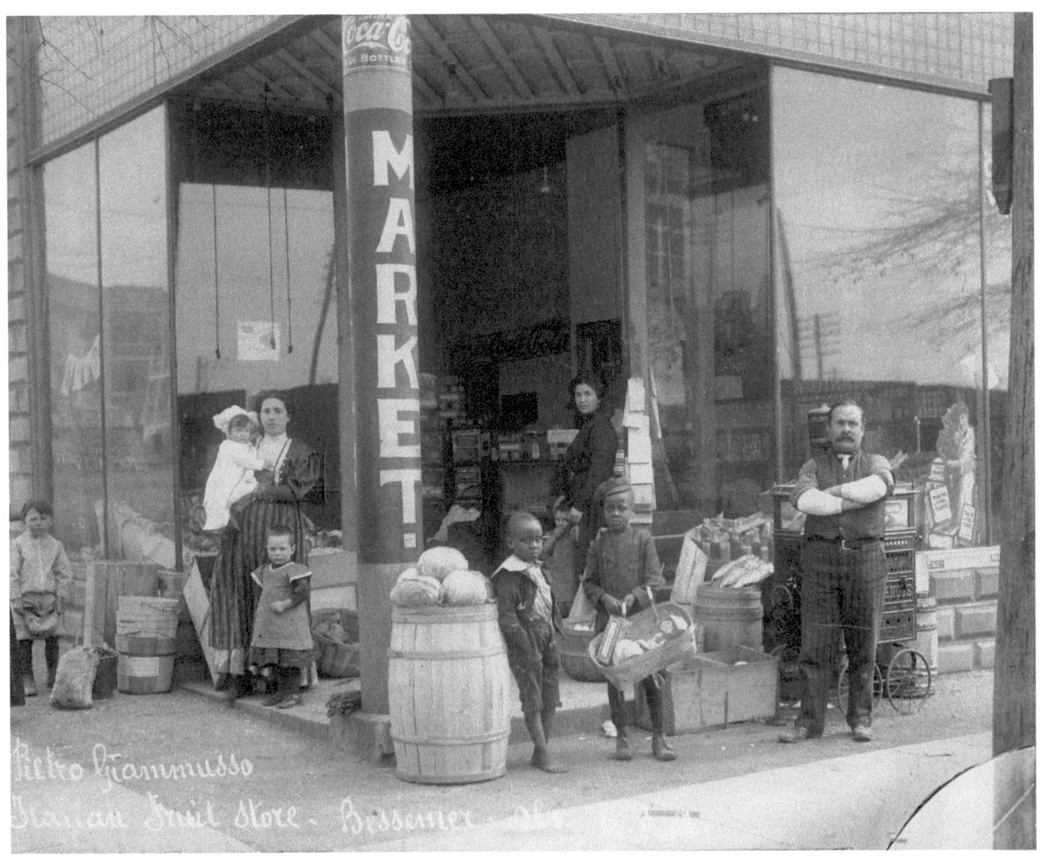

FIGURE 13*
Pietro Giammusso,
Italian Fruit Store.
Bessemer, Alabama
Photograph by D. Pace, Birmingham
Date unknown
$7\frac{5}{8}$ x $9\frac{5}{8}$ inches

The Dillingham Commission's 1911 report states that there were 150 Italian Americans in Bessemer (a city southwest of Birmingham) and that two grocery stores were operated by Italian Americans "but are patronized largely by negroes." There is no evidence of a Pietro Giammusso in Bessemer, but according to the 1913 Bessemer City Directory, a Pietro Giangrossa operated a grocery store at 1831 Carolina Avenue. Current Google Street Views at this address show a store building whose inscription reads "1907" and that has a corner entrance and pillar, strongly suggesting that it is the same structure shown in this photograph.

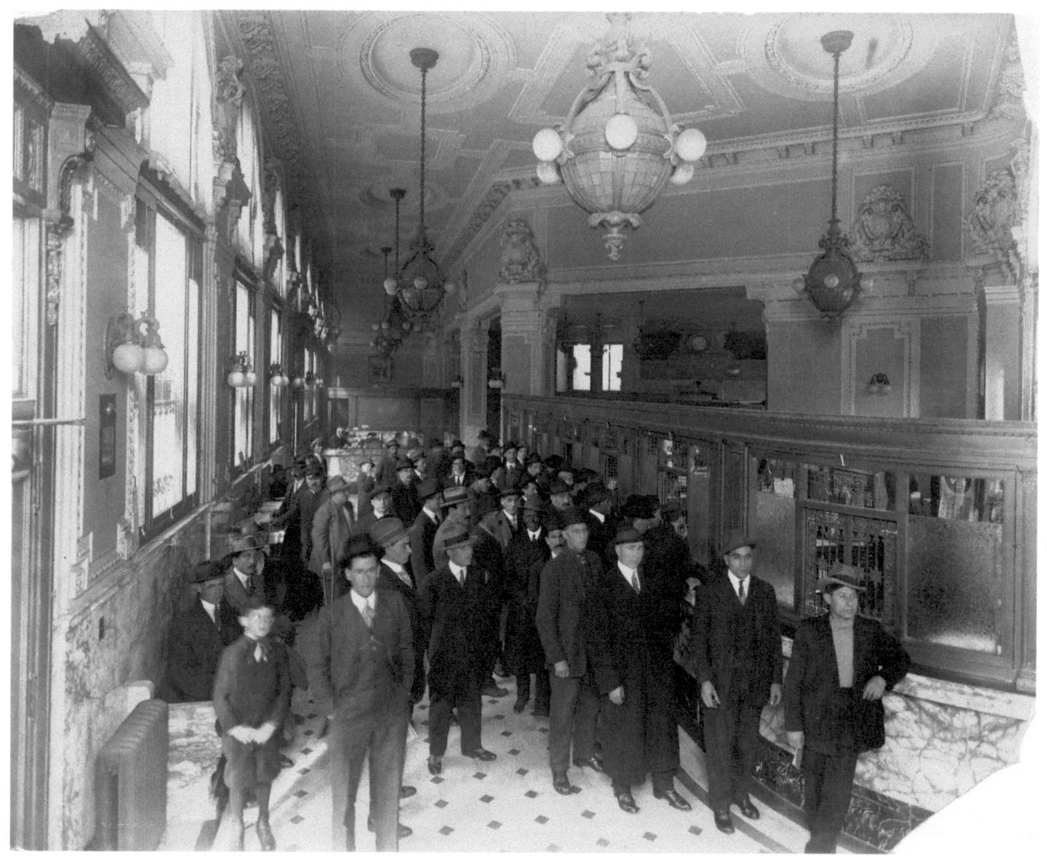

FIGURE 14*
Banca Popolare Fugazi
San Francisco, California
Photograph by Walter A. Scott, San Francisco
July 2, 1927
11 x 13¾ inches

Right: detail of back showing inscription

Giovanni F. "John" Fugazi immigrated to the United States in 1855 and opened the Banca Colombo in San Francisco in 1893. In 1906, he opened a new bank, the Banca Popolare Operaia Italiana, later renamed the Banca Popolare Fugazi. The bank building depicted here was constructed in 1909 and is now a San Francisco landmark. It has housed the Church of Scientology since 2003.

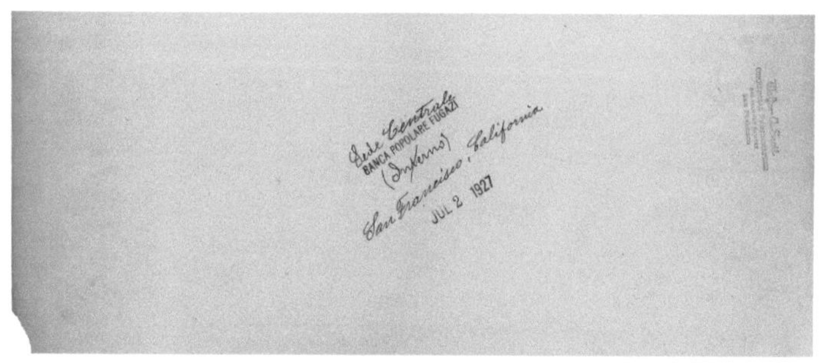

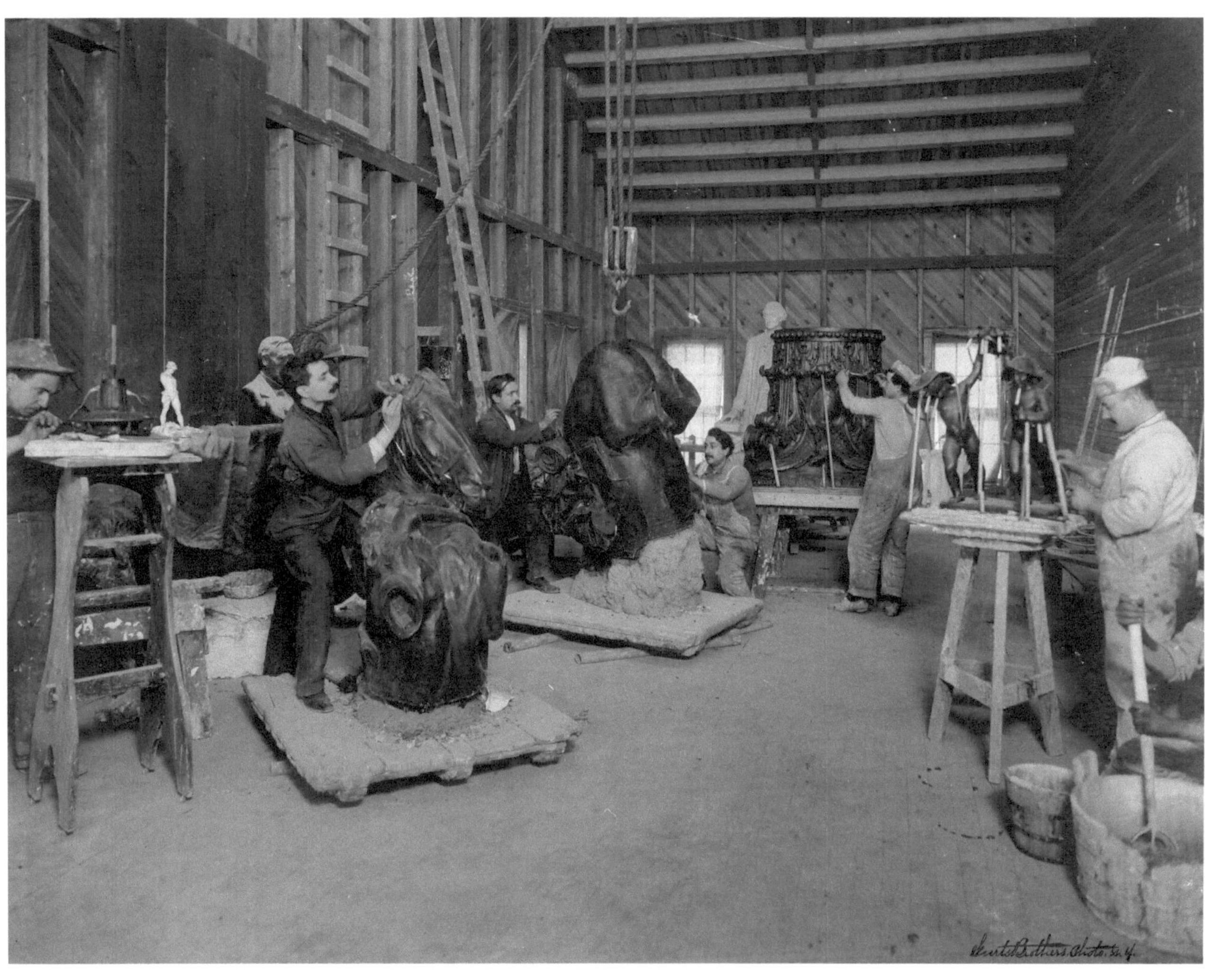

FIGURE 15*
Roman Bronze Works
"Messa in forma e ritoccatura delle cere."
[Molding and retouching the wax.]
275–289 Greene Street, Brooklyn, New York
Photograph by Wurts Brothers, New York
Date unknown
10 x 13 inches

Immigrant Riccardo Bertelli established Roman Bronze Works—the first American foundry to specialize in lost-wax casting (*cire-perdue*)—in 1899. Among the major American artists to work with the foundry are Frederic Remington and Charles M. Russell. In 1927, Roman Bronze Works relocated to Corona, Queens. The company remained active until the late 1980s, although not at the Corona studio.

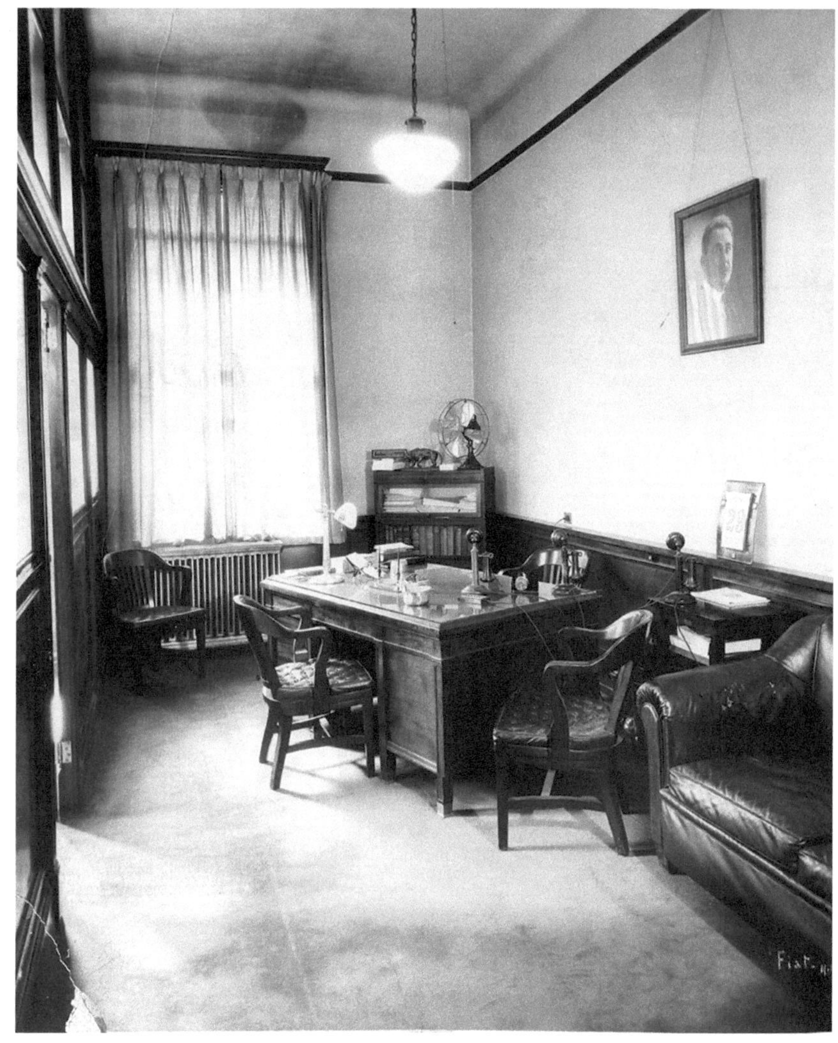

FIGURE 16*
Office of the President, Banco di Sicilia Trust Co.
New York, New York
Photographer unknown
Date unknown
16¾ x 14 inches

The Banco di Sicilia Trust Co. was founded in 1925 and renamed the Bank of Sicily Trust Co. four years later. The Banco di Napoli Trust Co. acquired the bank in 1936.

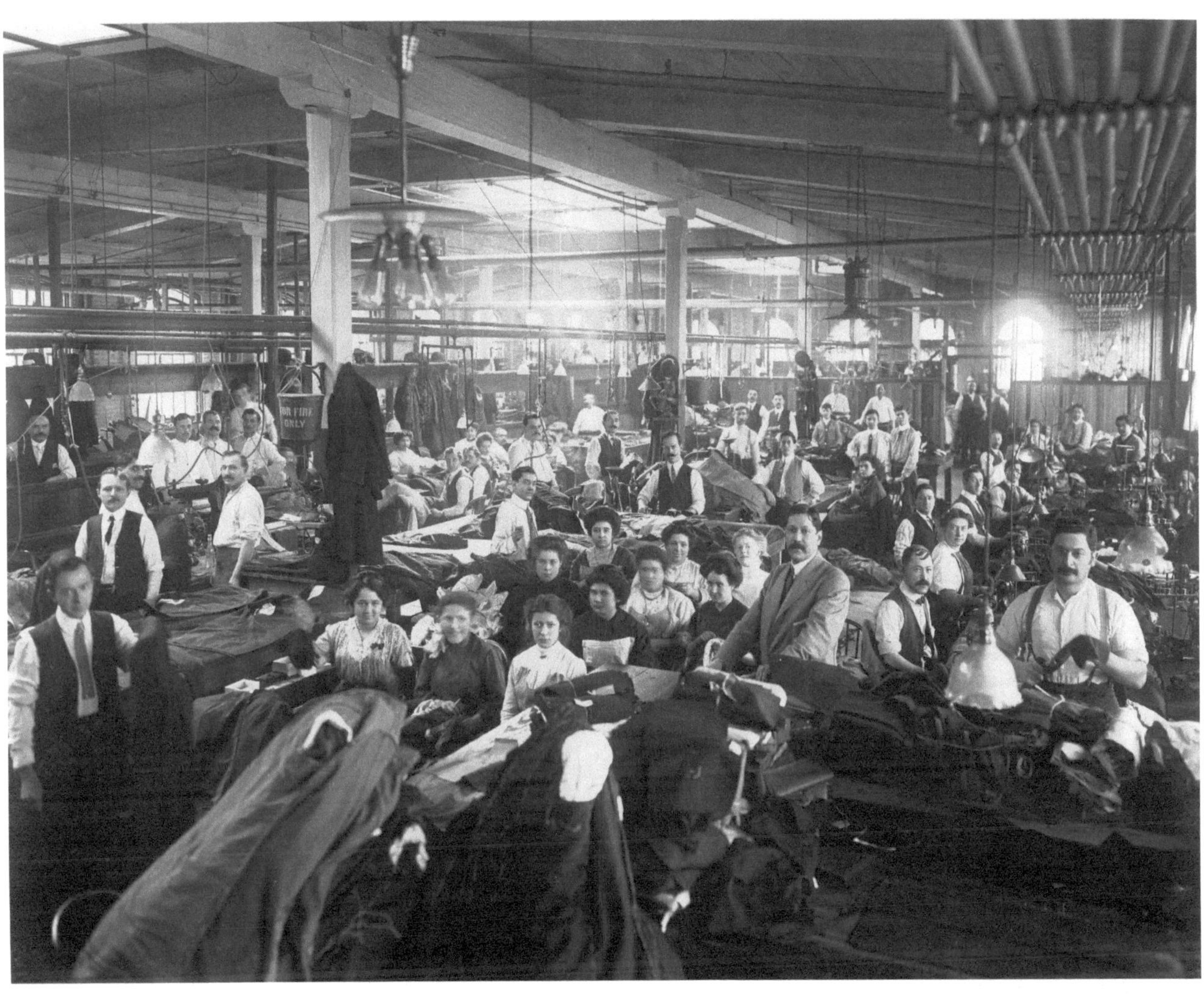

FIGURE 17*
Snellenburg Clothing Factory
"Reparto Sarti e Sarte Italiani"
[Department of Italian Tailors and Seamstresses]
Philadelphia, Pennsylvania
Photographer unknown
Date unknown
8¼ x 10¼ inches

Established in 1869, N. Snellenburg & Company was one of Philadelphia's leading department stores and wholesale clothing manufacturers. Its factory complex at 642 North Broad Street consists of two buildings, one constructed in 1903 and another built in 1905. In 1986 the factory was added to the National Register of Historic Places.

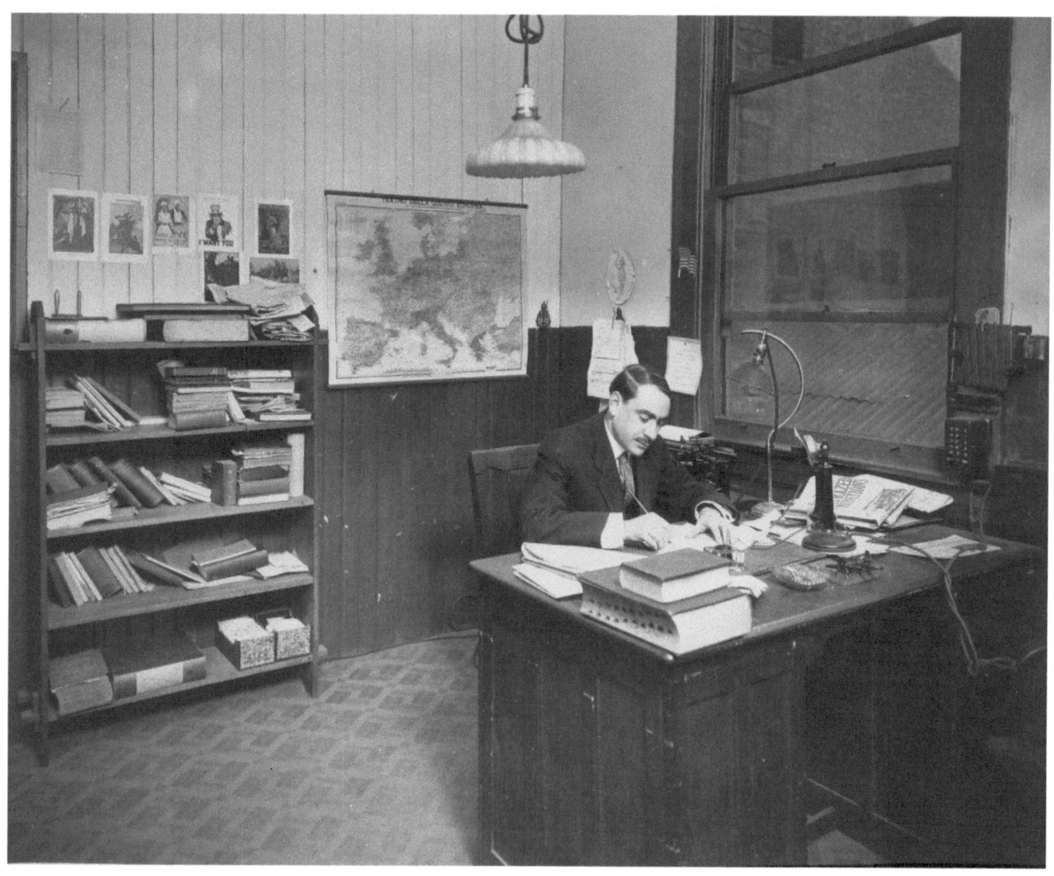

FIGURE 18*
An editorial room at
the newspaper *L'Italia*
San Francisco, California
Photograph by R.J. Waters & Co.,
San Francisco
Circa 1917
7¼ x 9 inches

The San Francisco-based *L'Italia* was established in 1886 and was active until 1965. Its most notable owner-editor was Ettore Patrizi. A supporter of Italian-American civic organizations and of opera in San Francisco, Patrizi extolled the virtues of North Beach as a "model Italian colony." In 1942, he was expelled from California by the U.S. Army's Western Defense Command due to his record of support for Fascism.

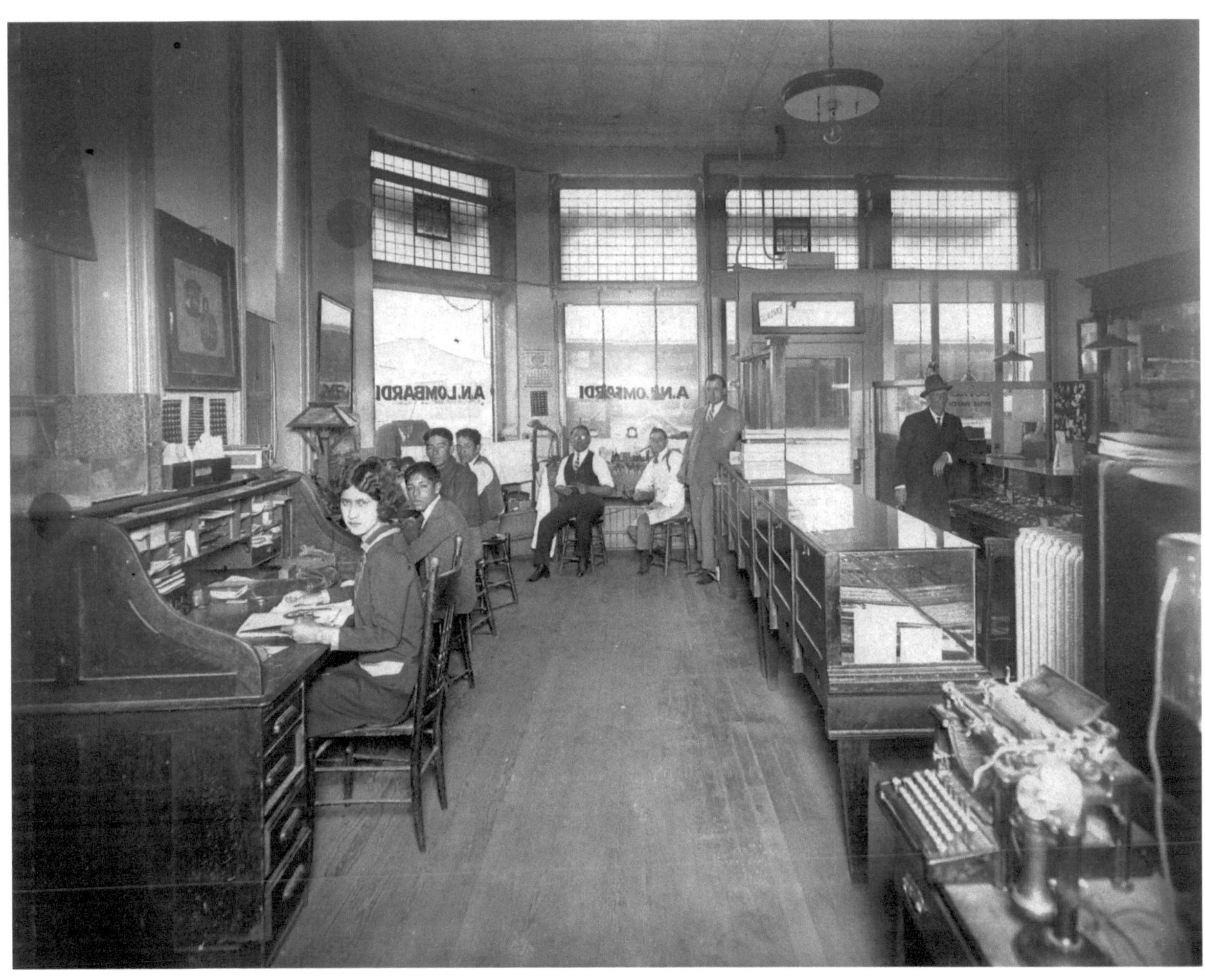

FIGURE 19*
A.N. Lombardi Jewelers
El Paso, Texas
Photographer unknown
Date unknown
6 1/8 x 8 1/8 inches

Angelo Nicholas Lombardi, an immigrant from Crecchio (Chieti province, Abruzzo), opened his El Paso jewelry business in 1913. A label below the photograph indicates that it was sent by the Italian Consulate in New Orleans.

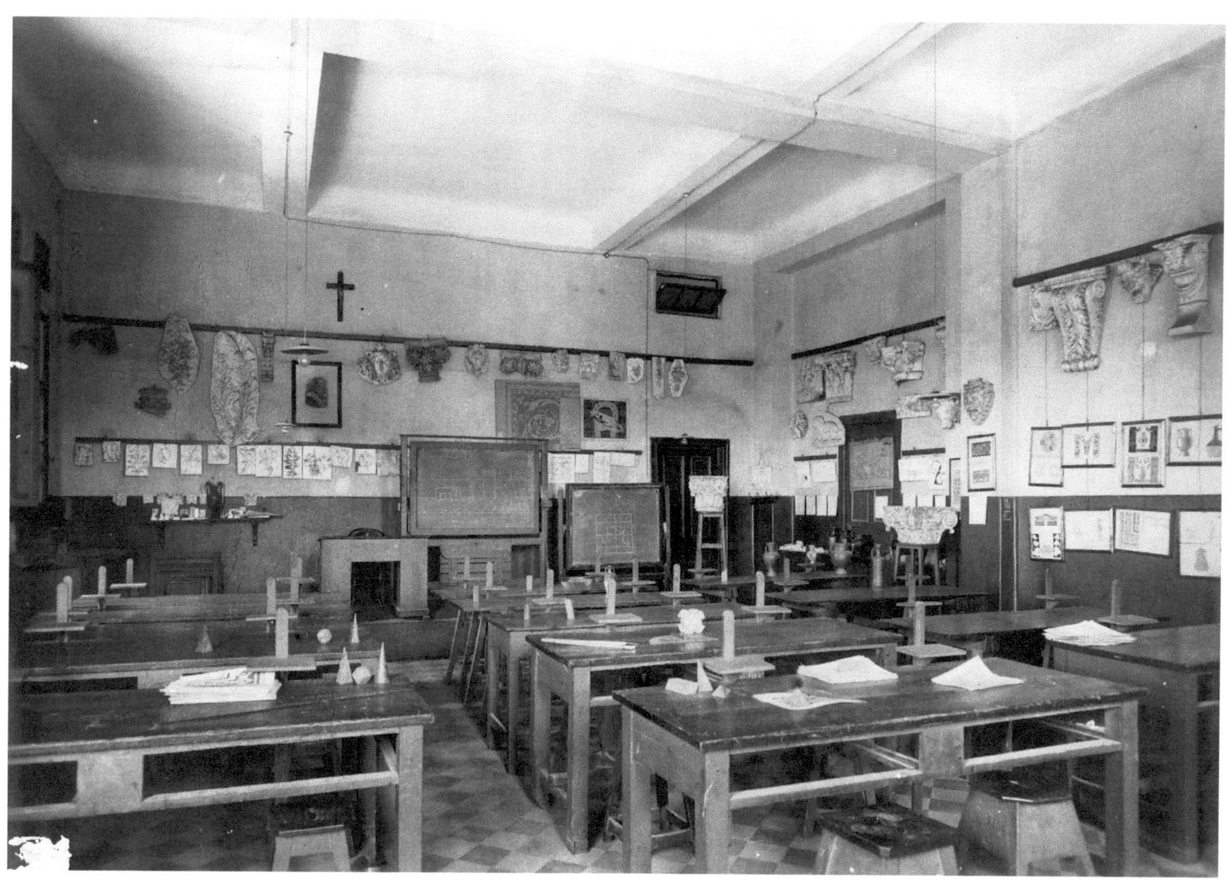

FIGURE 20
"R.R. Scuole Medie–Sala di disegno–Cairo" [Royal Middle School–Art classroom–Cairo]
Photograph by A. Del Vecchio
Date unknown
10 3/8 x 15 1/8 inches

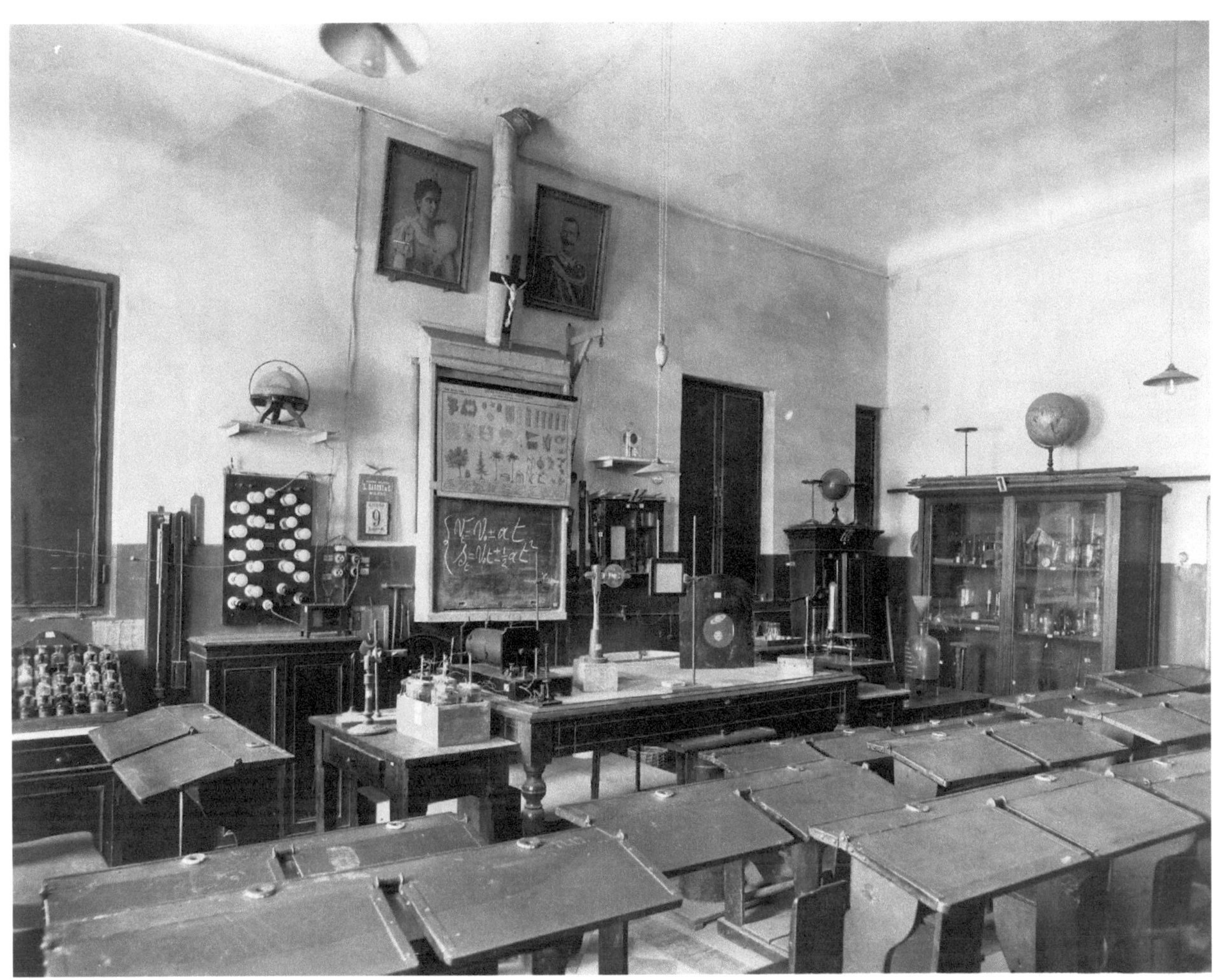

FIGURE 21
"R.R. Scuole Medie—Gabinetto di fisica e chimica—Cairo" [Royal Middle School—Physics and chemistry classroom—Cairo]
Photograph by A. Del Vecchio
Date unknown
11½ x 15¼ inches

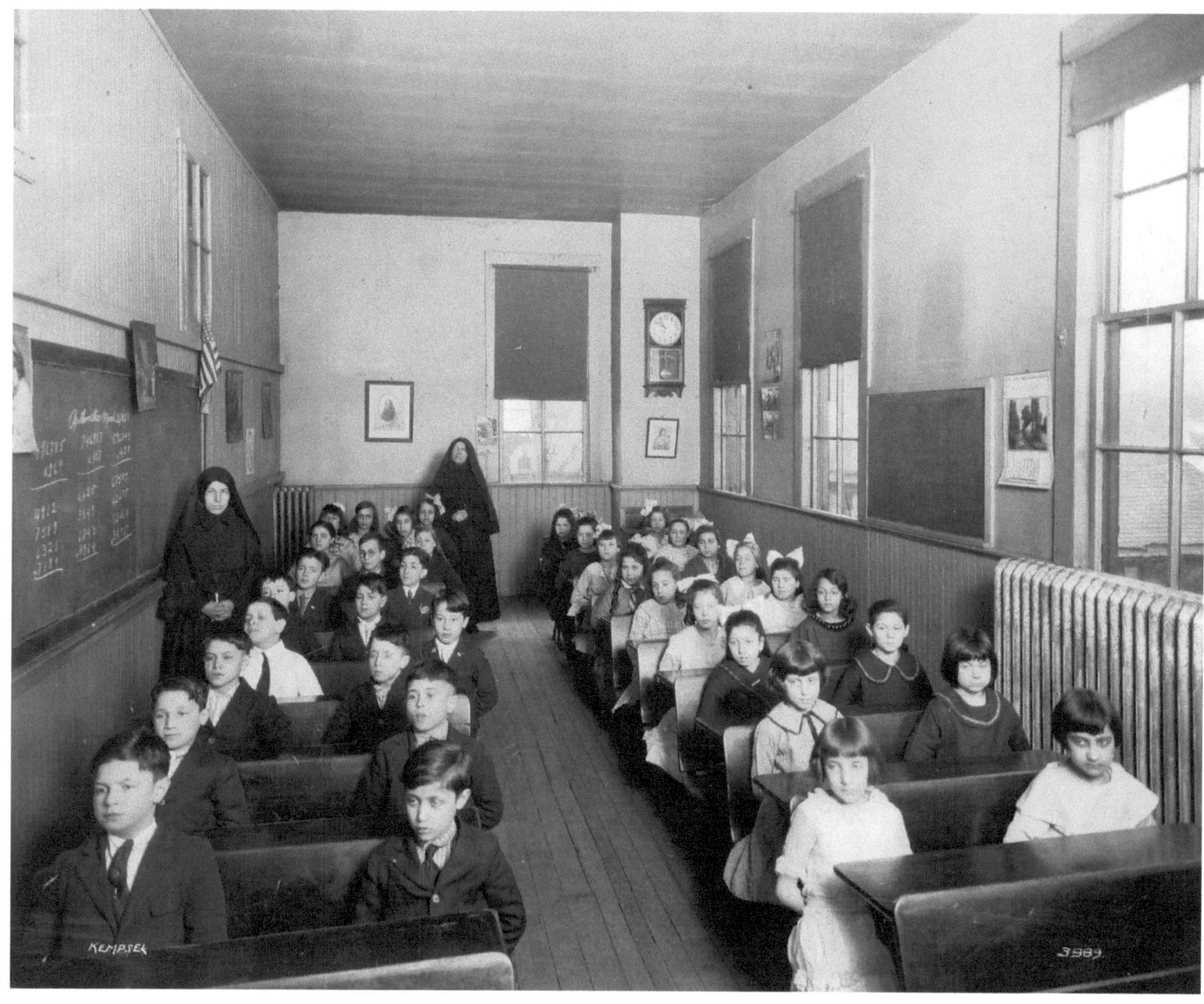

FIGURE 22
School of the Missionary Sisters of the Sacred Heart, Third Grade.
Scranton, Pennsylvania
Photograph by Kempsel
Date unknown
$7^{1/2}$ x $9^{3/8}$ inches

This appears to be a photo of St. Frances Xavier Cabrini School, founded in 1901 and staffed by Mother Cabrini's Missionary Sisters of the Sacred Heart. Mother Cabrini made multiple trips to Scranton to help establish the school and the parish of St. Lucy's Church, officially designated the "Mother Italian Church" of the Diocese of Scranton. The building was formerly Public School 16; today it houses apartments for senior citizens.

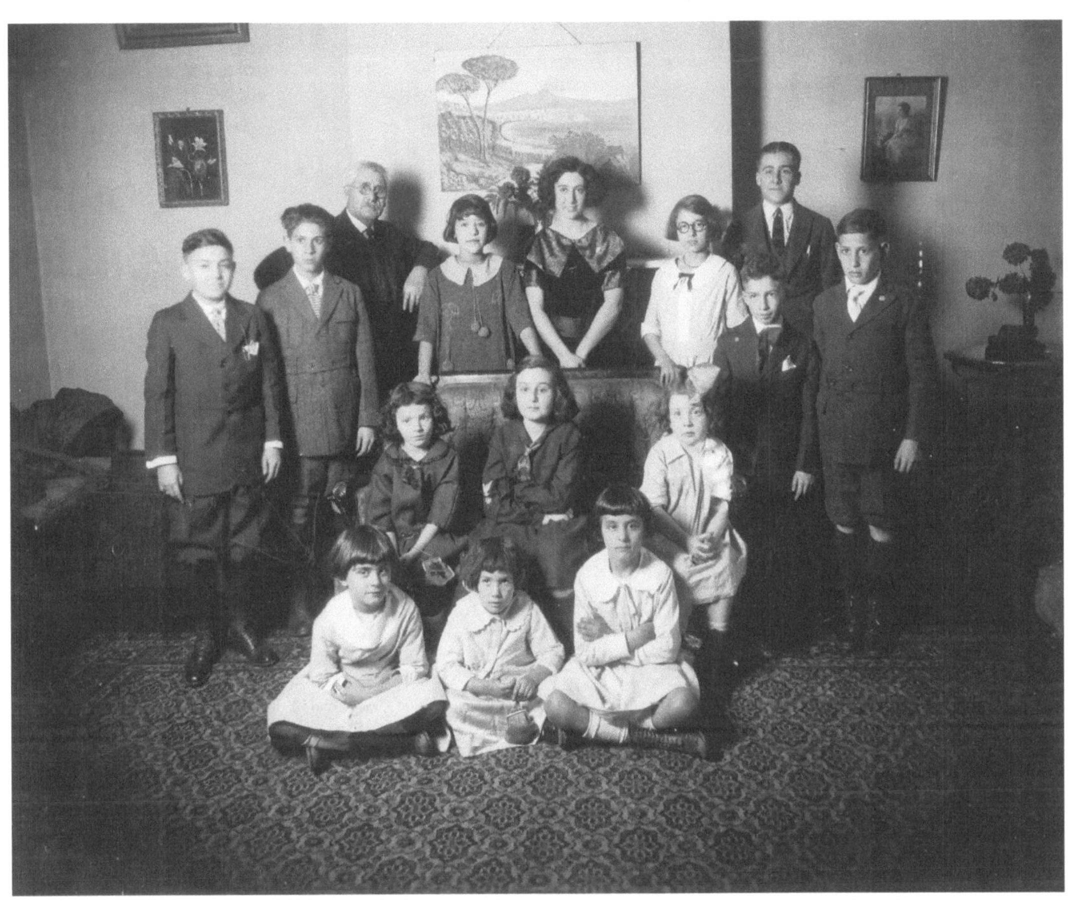

FIGURE 23*
"Scuola Italiana Dante"
Savannah, Georgia
Photographer unknown
Date unknown
7 x 8¾ inches

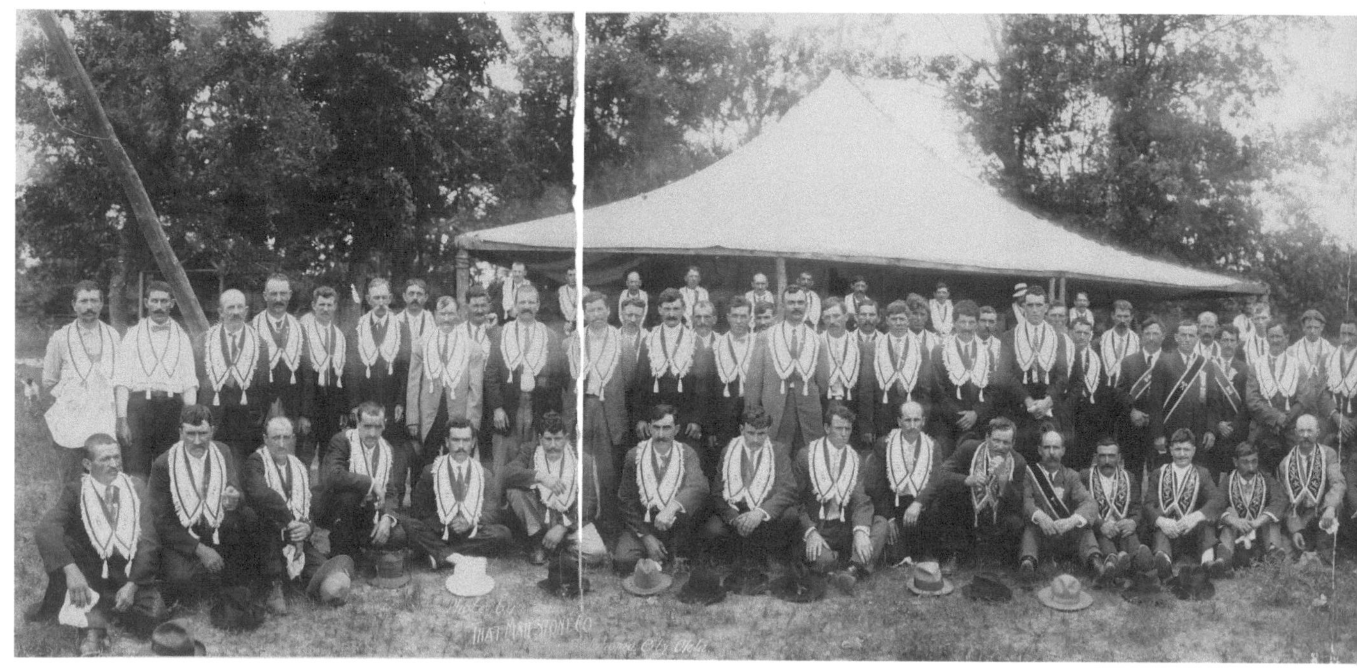

FIGURE 24
Sixth Anniversary of Dante Lodge No. 523,
Independent Order of Odd Fellows
Alderson, Oklahoma
Photograph by That Man Stone Co.,
Oklahoma City
June 4, 1915
10 x 42 inches

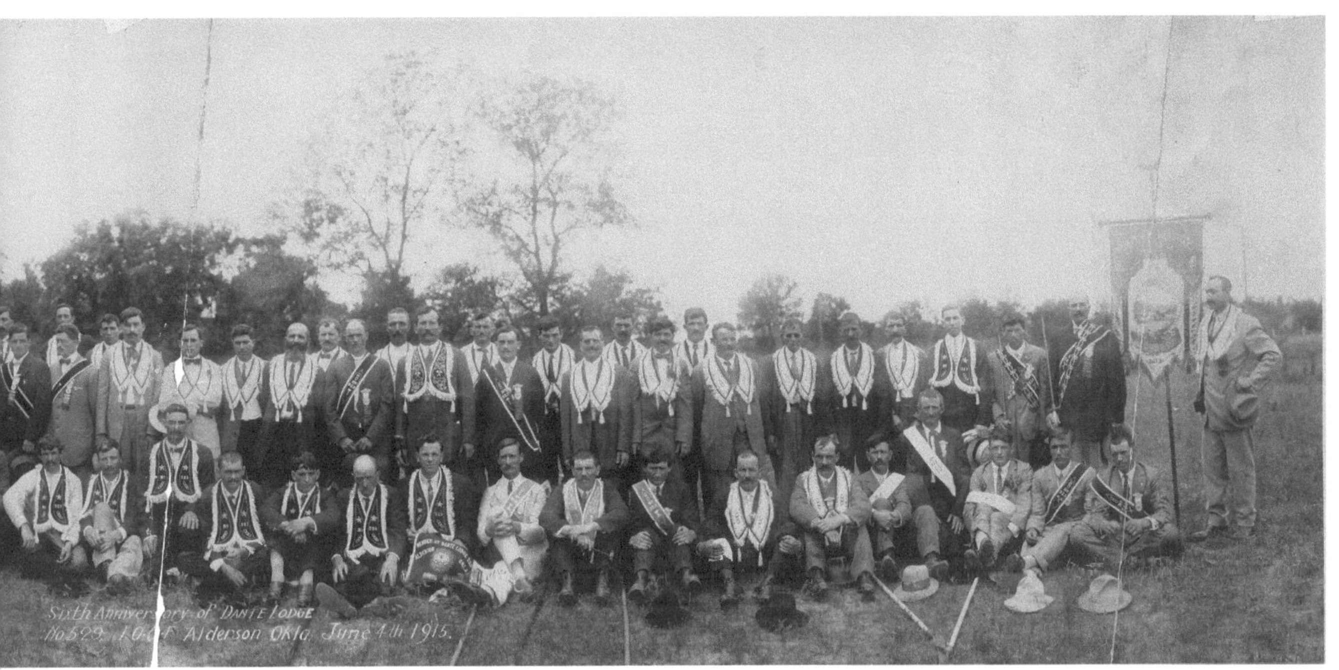

Coal mines drew Italian immigrants to southeastern Oklahoma, where they settled in towns such as Alderson, Krebs, and McAlester. That Man Stone Co. was a major Oklahoma City photography studio founded by Fred L. Stone. The Independent Order of Odd Fellows was a fraternal organization with roots in eighteenth-century England.

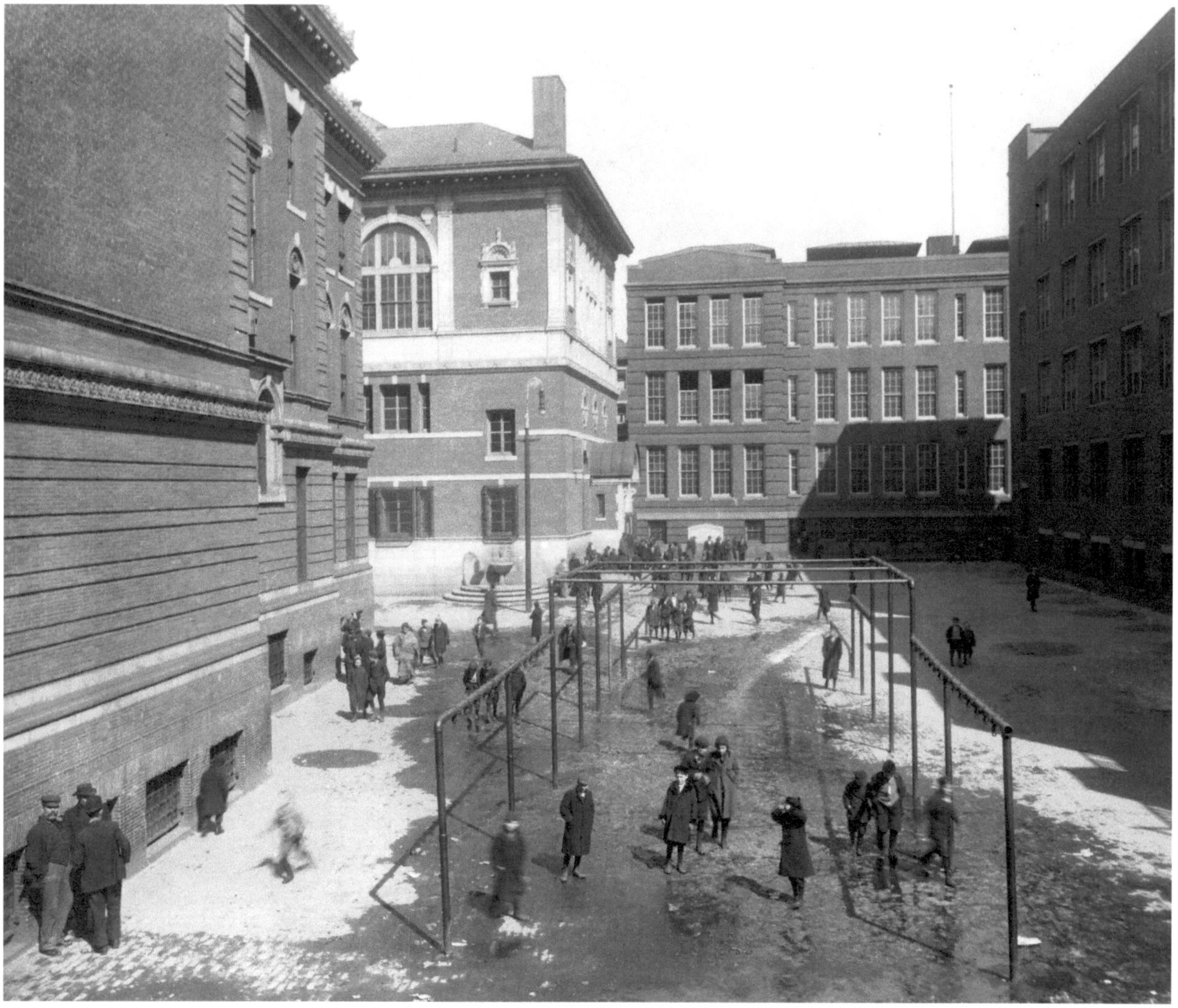

FIGURE 25*
"Scuola Cristoforo Colombo—Piazzale con palestra—Quartiere Italiano" [Christopher Columbus School—Plaza with gymnasium—Italian neighborhood]
Boston, Massachusetts
Photograph by Dadmun, Boston
Date unknown
7½ x 9 inches

Right: matted photograph

The Christopher Columbus School on Tileston Street in Boston's North End was completed in 1903. The school closed in the 1990s, and the building was converted into condominiums. This photograph appears to be taken at what is now Polcari Playground, looking toward the rear of the school.

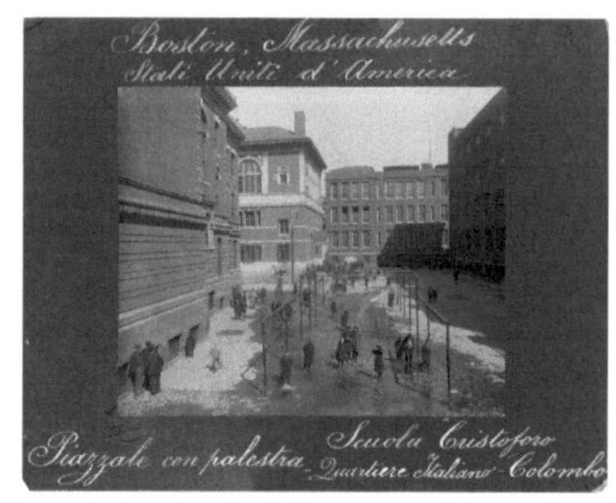

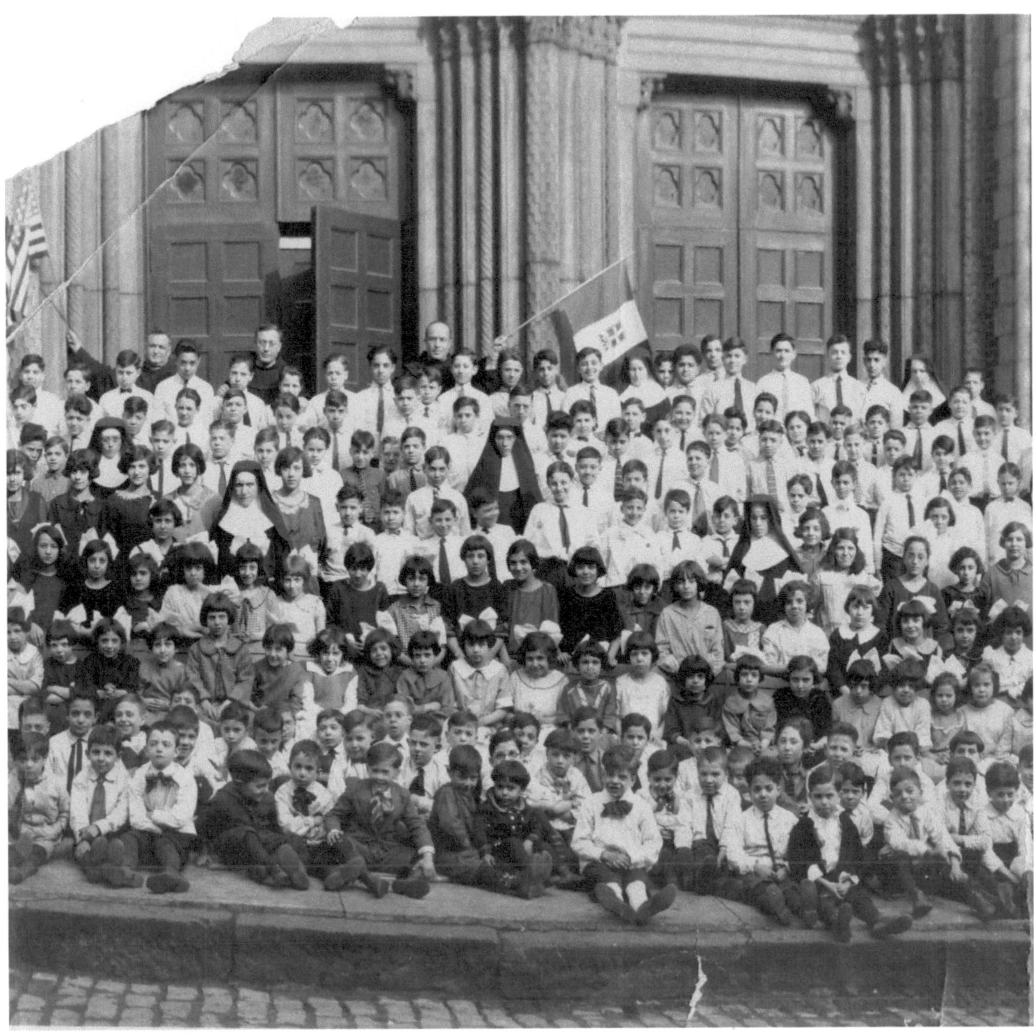

FIGURE 26*
St. Peter's Church, Fernando Street
Pittsburgh, Pennsylvania
Photographer unknown
Date unknown
9¼ x 9¾ inches

St. Peter's Church served the Italian Americans of the Lower Hill District in Pittsburgh. The building depicted in this photograph was dedicated in 1918. In 1960, the city's Urban Redevelopment Authority razed the church to make room for the Chatham Center, a commercial and residential complex. Much of the surrounding area, deemed a slum by city authorities, met the same fate.

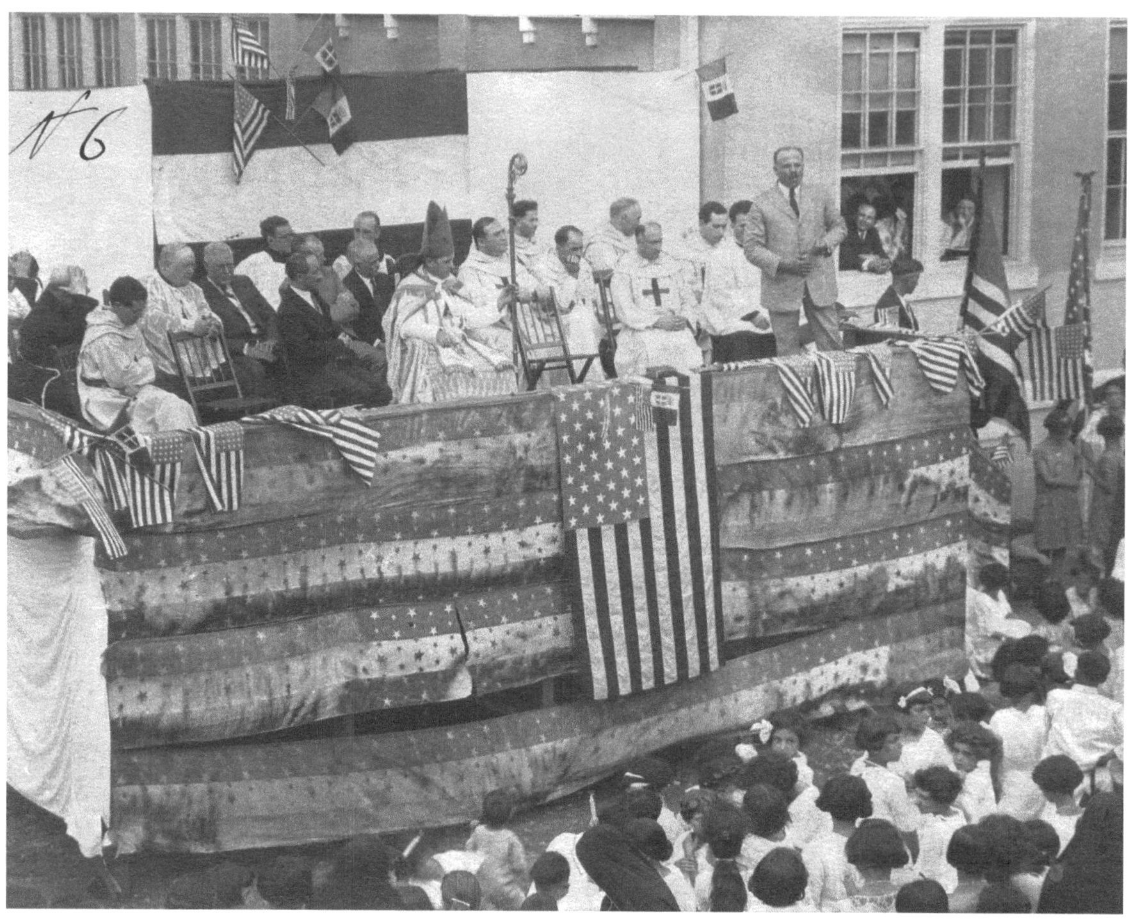

FIGURE 27*

"Inaugurazione della Scuola della Chiesa di S. Anna: Oratore il sig. Angelo di Renzo contrattore /R. Ambasciata d'Italia in Washington." [Inauguration of the school of the Church of St. Ann: Speaker Mr. Angelo di Renzo contractor/Royal Embassy of Italy in Washington.]
Bristol, Pennsylvania
Photograph by The Nichols Studio, Bristol
1925
7½ x 9½ inches

St. Ann's School in Bristol was started in the St. Ann's Church convent in 1920. In 1925, the three-story school building pictured here opened on Logan Street. According to the inscriptions on the photograph, builder Angelo di Renzo is shown addressing the crowd. Di Renzo was a Bristol-based contractor active in Bucks County.

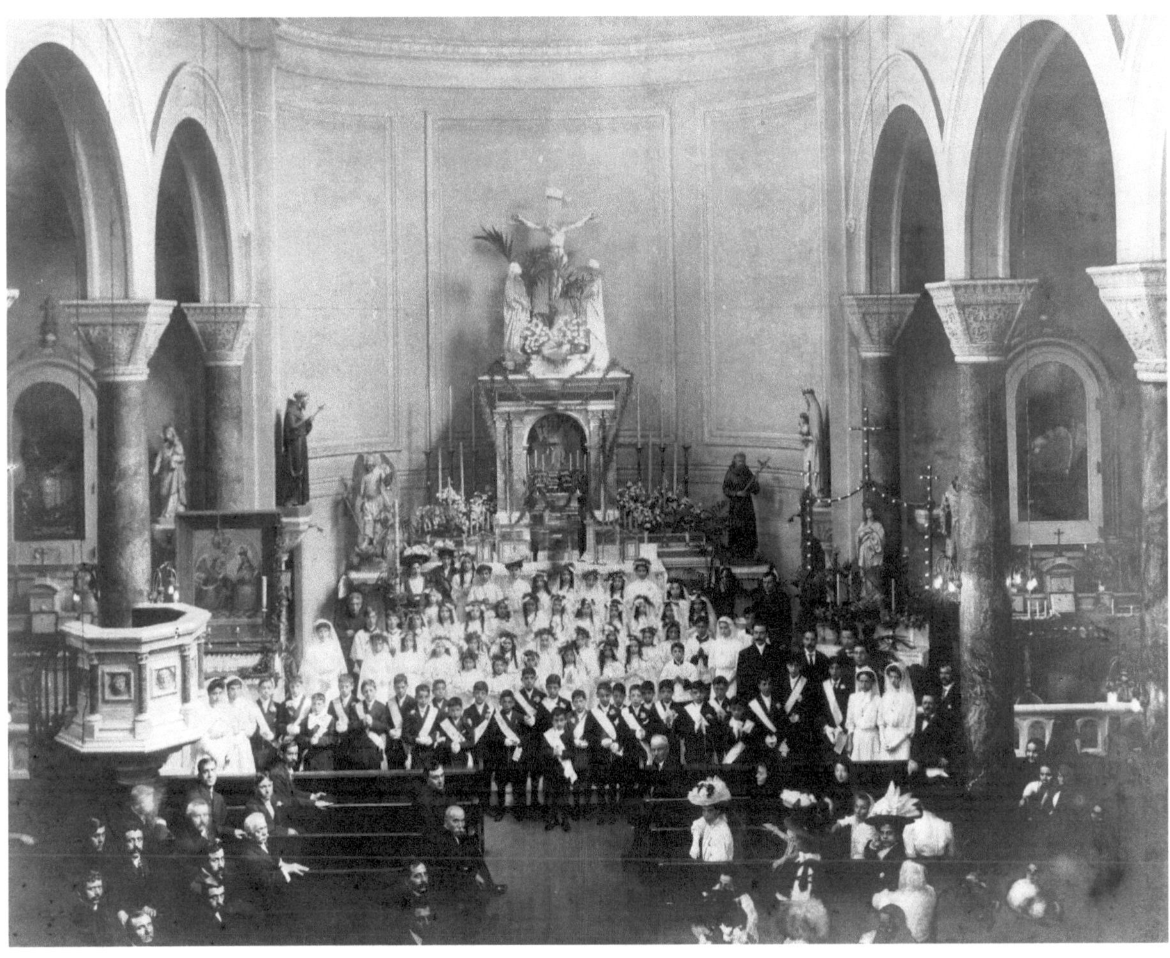

FIGURE 28
Church of the Most Precious Blood
New York, New York
Photograph by R. Tebbs
Date unknown
8 7/8 x 11 1/8 inches

Located on Baxter Street in Manhattan's Little Italy, the Church of the Most Precious Blood was established as an Italian national parish in 1888 but was not completed until 1891. It would eventually be designated the National Shrine of San Gennaro (St. Januarius). It underwent a major renovation in 1995 and was merged twenty years later with Old St. Patrick's Cathedral. Its current parishioners are predominantly Vietnamese Americans.

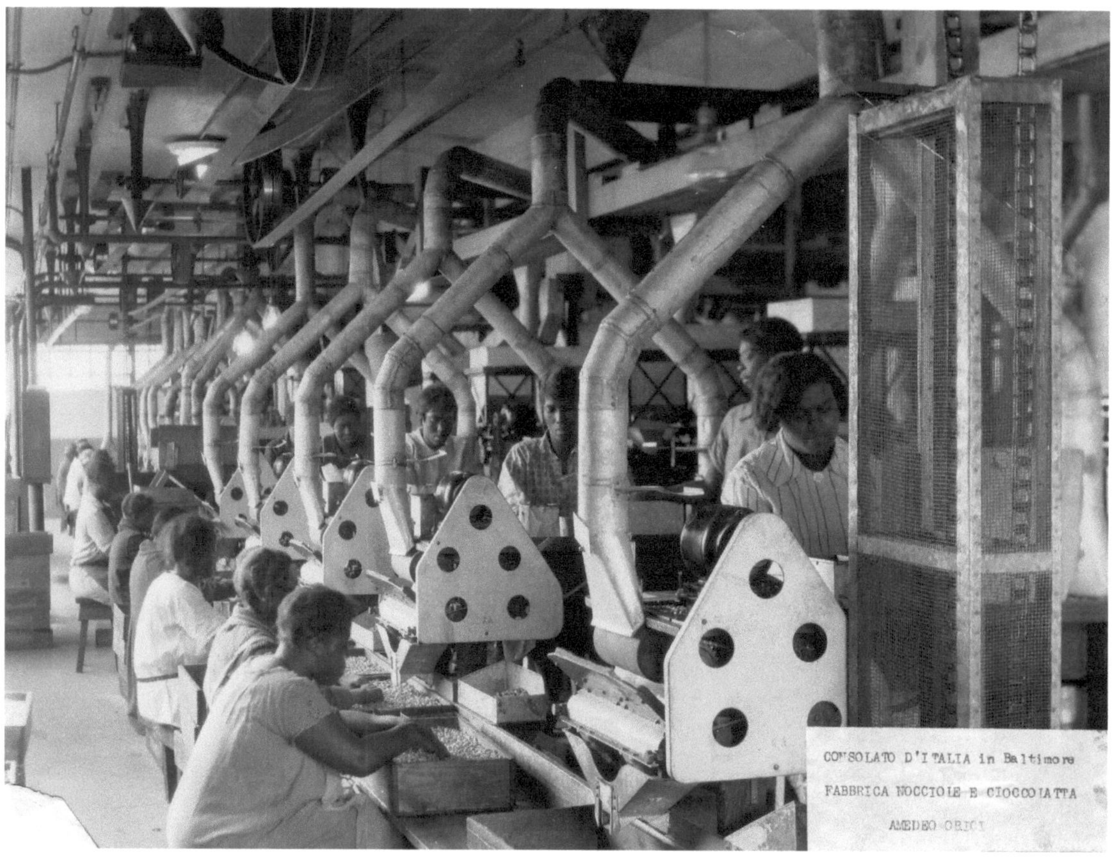

FIGURE 29
Planters Nut and Chocolate Company
Suffolk, Virginia
Photograph by Hamblin Studio, Suffolk
Date unknown
9 x 11 5/8 inches

Italian immigrant Amedeo Obici founded Planters in 1906 in Wilkes-Barre, Pennsylvania, with his business partner Mario Peruzzi. In 1913, Obici established a mass processing plant in Suffolk, Virginia. Suffolk's Hamblin Studio was active throughout the twentieth century, and its photograph collection is housed at the Suffolk Public Library. A label below the photograph indicates that it was sent by the Italian Consulate in Baltimore.

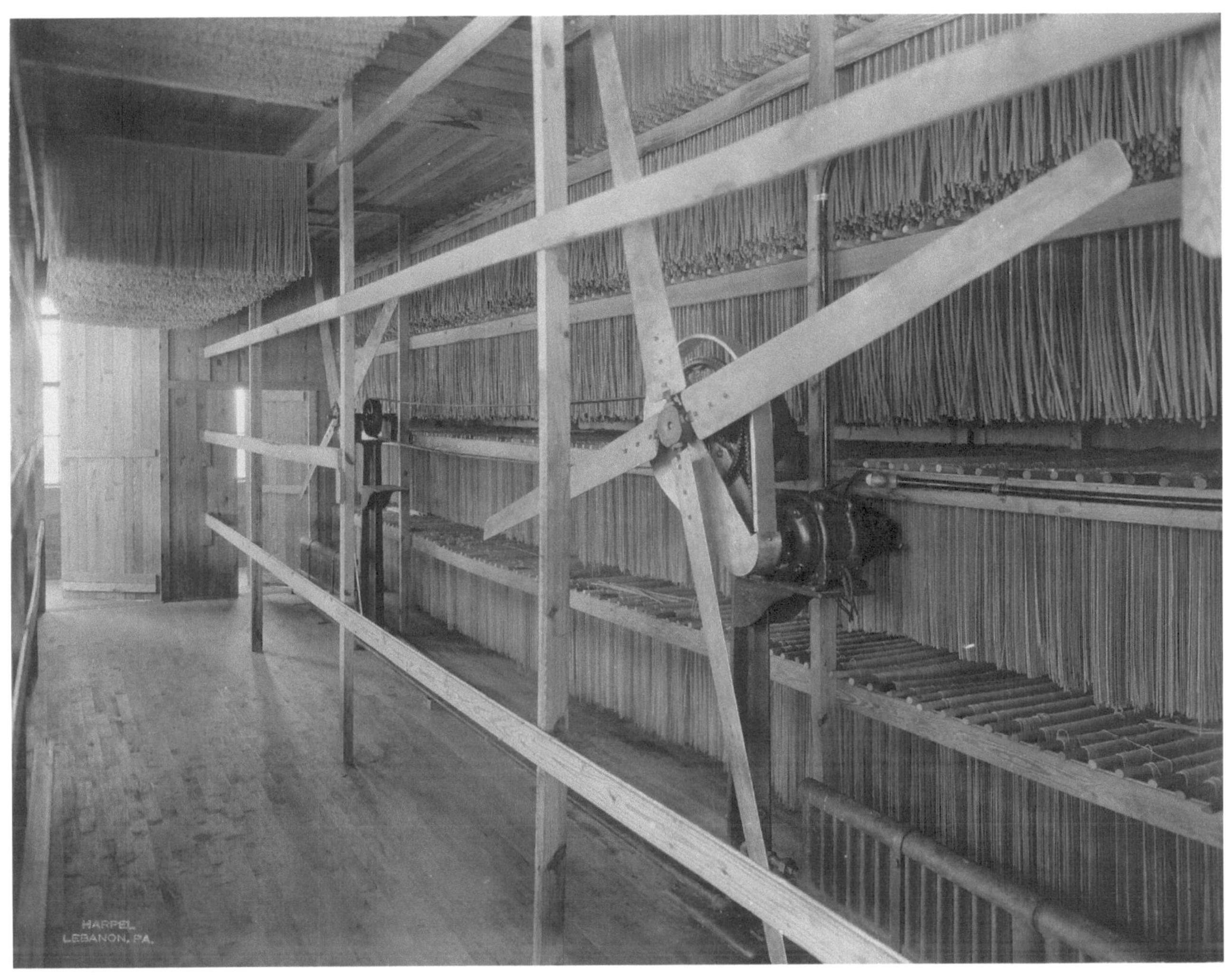

FIGURE 30
Spaghetti drying at the Keystone Macaroni Manufacturing Company
Lebanon, Pennsylvania
Photograph by Harpel
Date unknown
7 3/8 x 9 1/2 inches

This photograph is part of an album documenting the Keystone Macaroni Manufacturing Company. Girolami Guerrisi founded the company in 1914, having taken over what was originally a one-man operation. It was renamed the San Giorgio Macaroni Company in 1947. The plant was leveled by a fire in 1960. San Giorgio is now part of the New World Pasta family of brands.

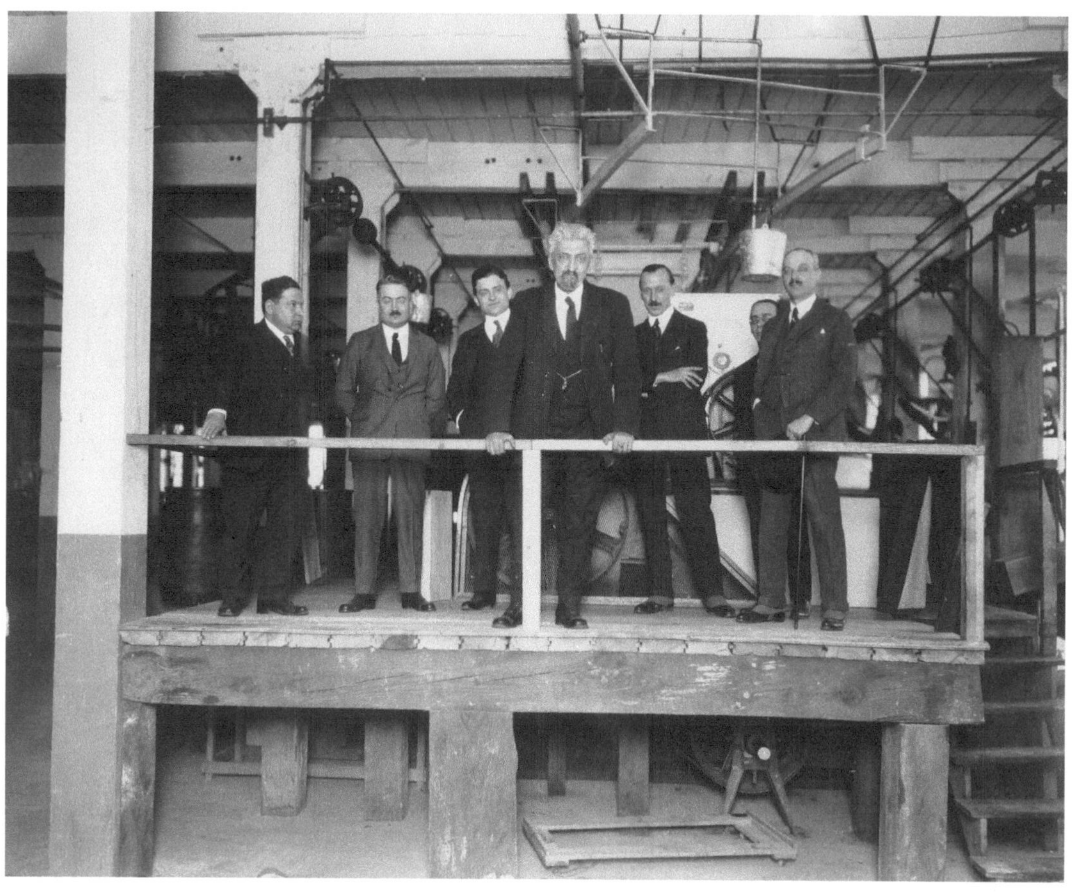

FIGURE 31
Keystone Macaroni Manufacturing Company
Lebanon, Pennsylvania
Photograph by Harpel
Circa 1923
$7^{3/8} \times 9^{1/2}$

Another photograph in the album documenting the Keystone Macaroni Manufacturing Company, the "Onorevole Podrecca" is Guido Podrecca, Socialist-turned-Fascist and co-founder of the weekly satirical journal *L'Asino*, started in Rome. He died of bronchopneumonia in Auburn, New York, during his propaganda tour.

Text on back:

"L'Onorevole Podrecca/In una delle sue ultime arringhe durante il suo giro di Propaganda Fascista ne gli Stati Uniti, sorpreso dall'obbiettivo mentre parlava della Nuova Italia ad un gruppo di Operai della Fabbrica" [The Honorable Podrecca/In one of his final exhortations during his tour of Fascist Propaganda in the United States, in a candid moment while he spoke of the New Italy to a group of factory workers] Left to right: G. Guerrisi, president of the company; N. Latorraca; H. Scaramelli; G. Podrecca; E. Locatelli; J. Capolino; M. Vincenzi.

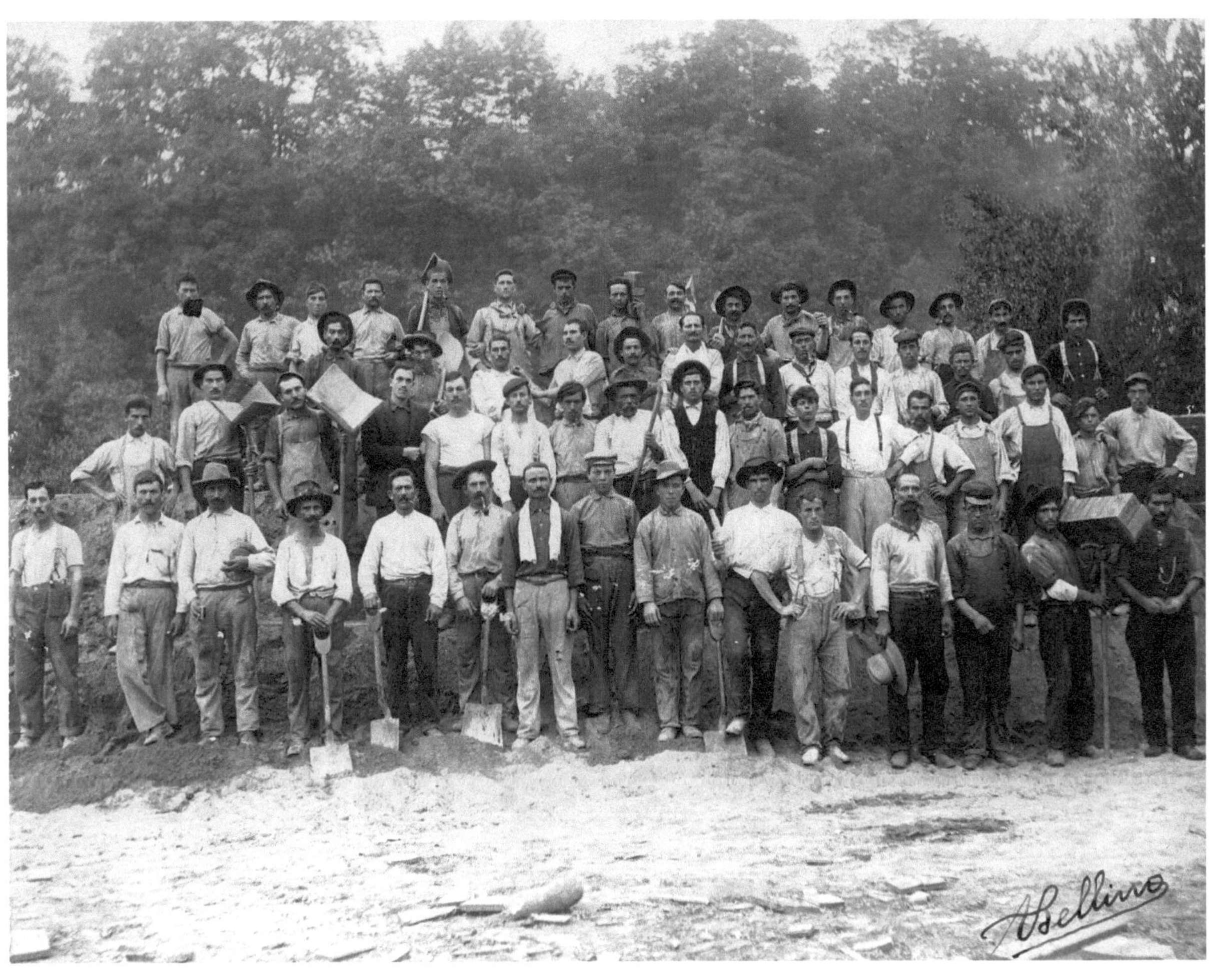

FIGURE 32*
"Gruppo lavoratori Italiani"
[Group of Italian workers]
Near Philadelphia, Pennsylvania
Photograph by A. Bellino
Date unknown
6 1/4 x 8 1/8 inches

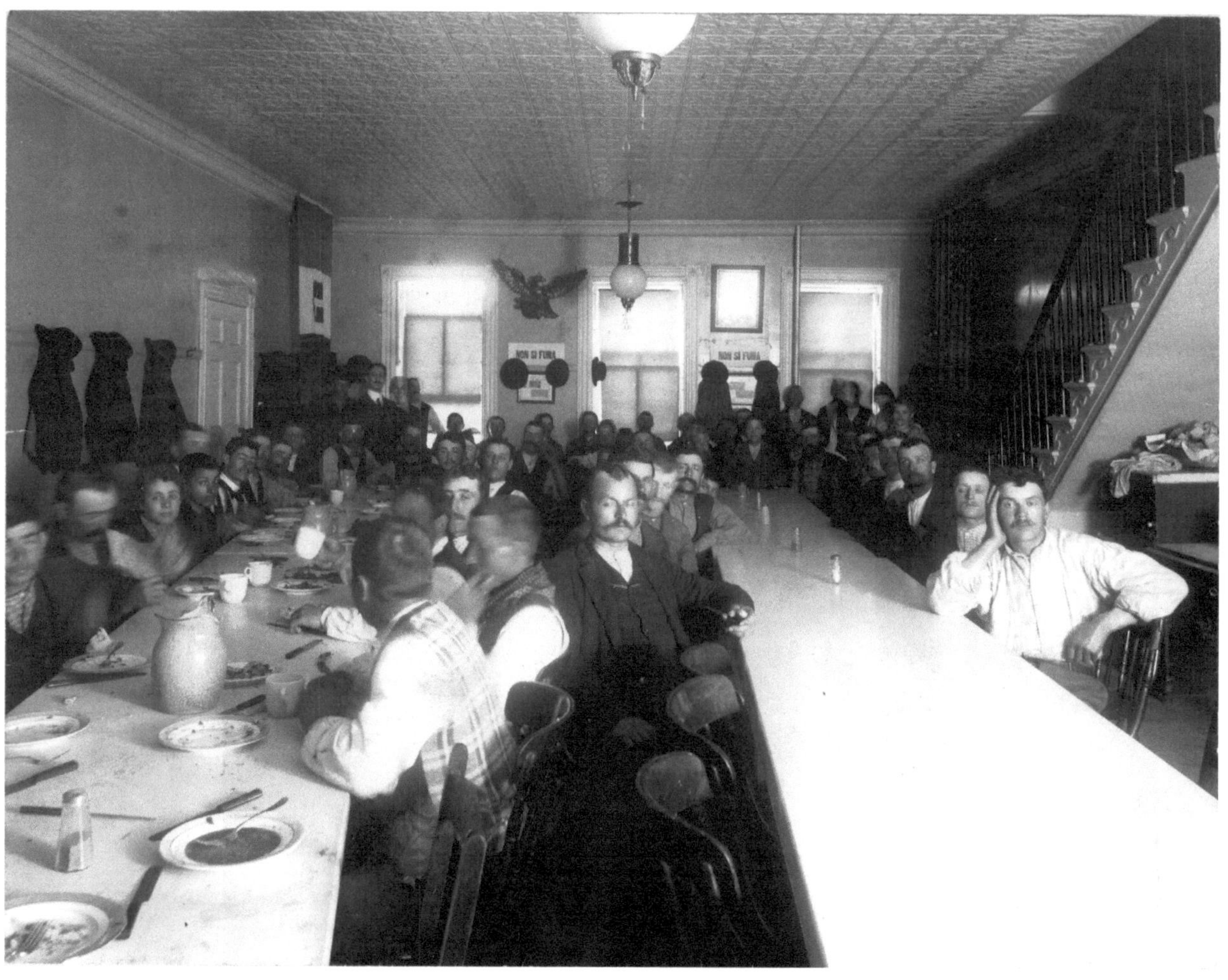

FIGURE 33
"Sede dell' Istituto italiano di beneficenza a Nuova York (West Houston Street N. 165–167) per la protezione degli immigranti italiani—Dormitorii e refettorio." [Headquarters of the Italian Benevolent Institute in New York (165–167 West Houston Street) for the protection of Italian immigrants—Dormitory and dining hall.]
New York, New York
Photographer unknown
Circa 1906
6 5/8 x 8 3/4 inches

This is one of four photographs mounted to a large board depicting the Italian Benevolent Institute, which was organized in 1857 and incorporated in 1882. The institute assisted poor Italian immigrants in New York City by providing food, lodging, and medical care.

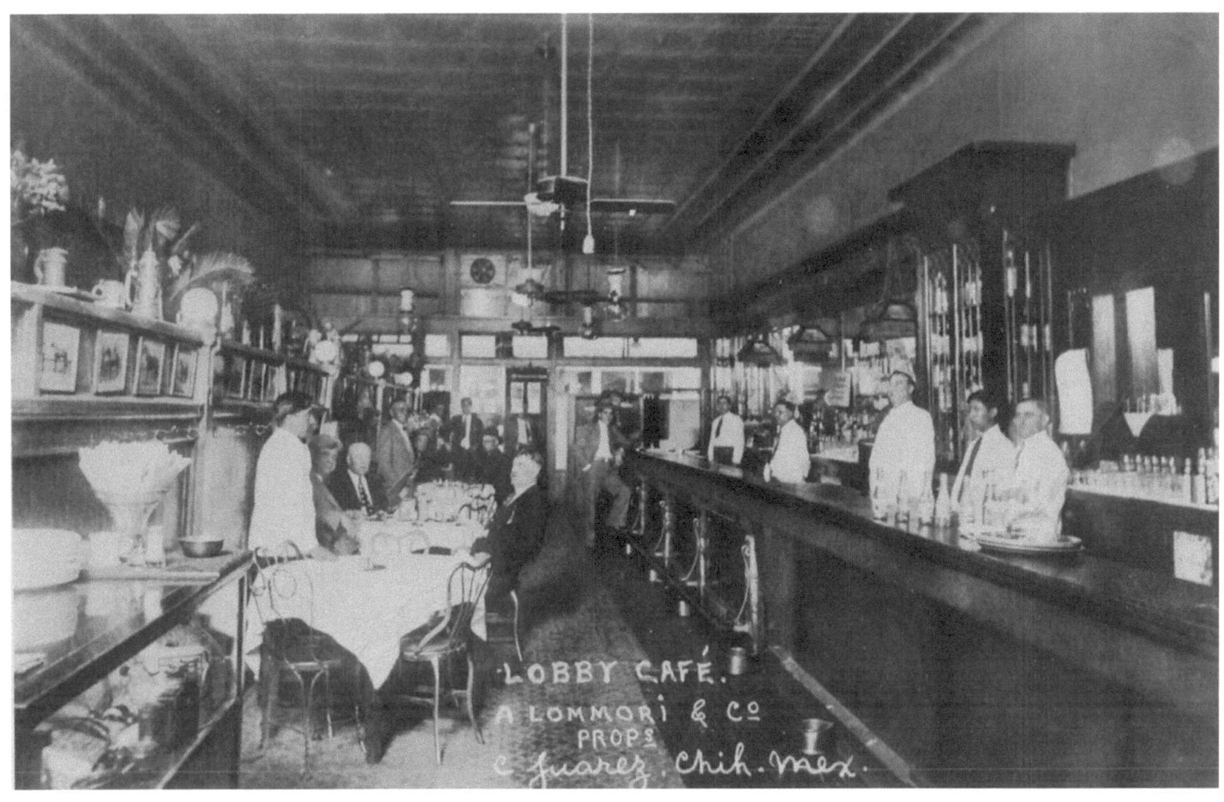

FIGURE 34
Lobby Café
A. Lommori & Co., Proprietors
Ciudad Juárez, Mexico
Photographer unknown
Date unknown
$3\frac{3}{8}$ x $5\frac{3}{8}$ inches

This photograph is mounted on paper along with a photograph of another Juárez café, the Gem Café ("Peter Barboglio, Proprietor"). Though both cafés are located in Juárez, the photographs are labeled in Italian the "Italian Community of El Paso." Another label indicates that the photographs were sent by the Italian Consulate in New Orleans.

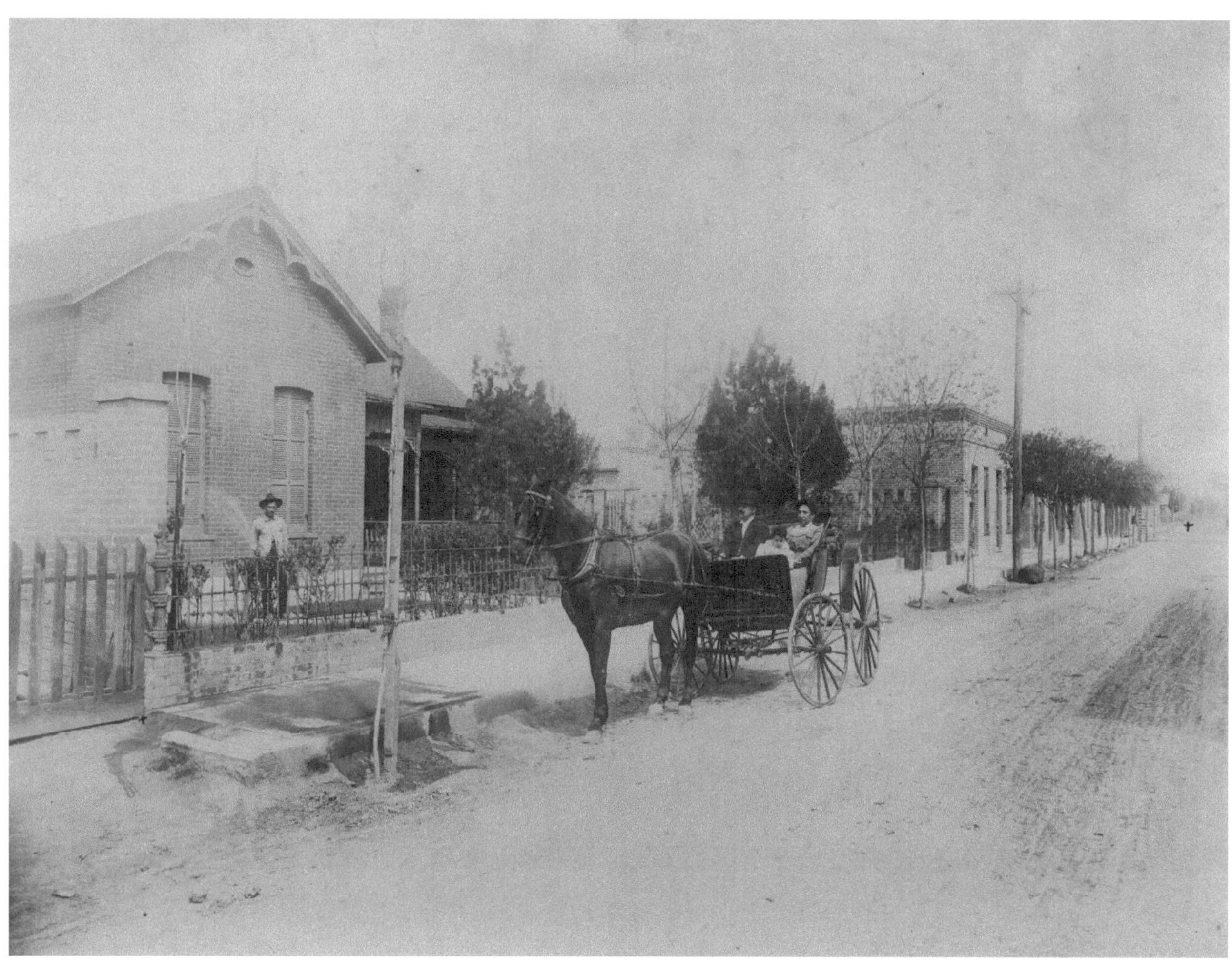

FIGURE 35
Rodolfo Zaffirini's home
Laredo, Texas
Photographer unknown
Date unknown
7 x 9 3/8 inches

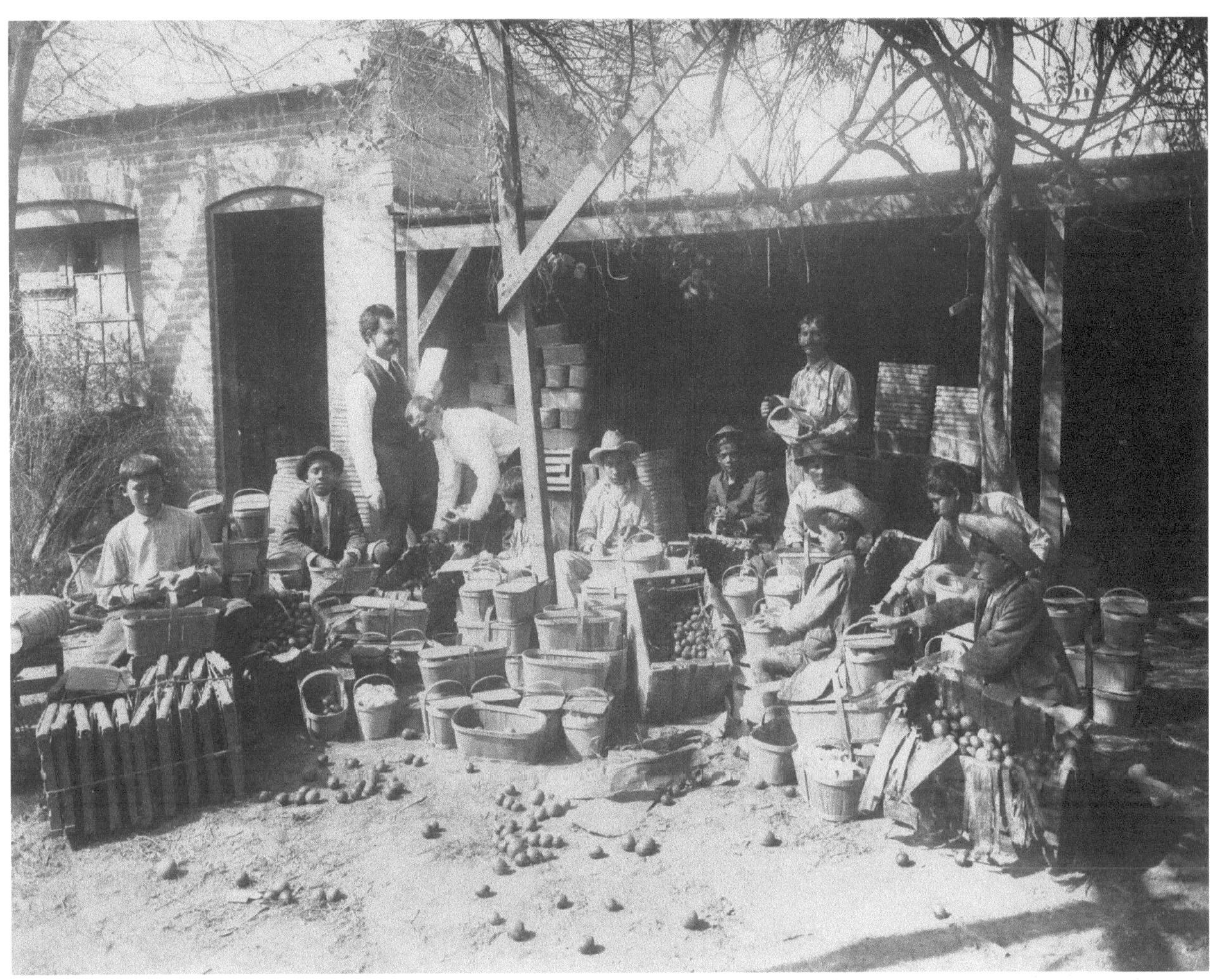

FIGURE 36
Zaffirini & Barberio
"Commercio di importazione ed esportazione di frutta ed altri prodotti messicani ed americani."
[Import and export of Mexican and American fruit and other products.]
Laredo, Texas
Photographer unknown
Date unknown
7¼ x 9¼ inches

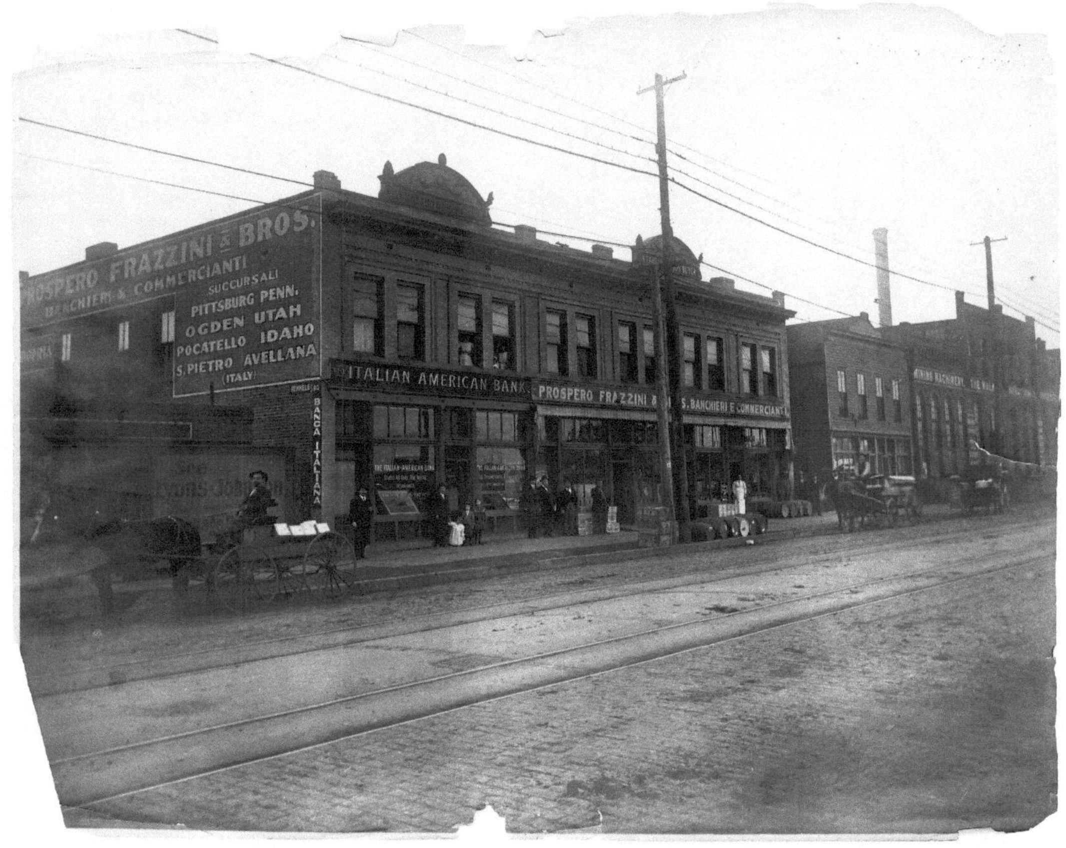

FIGURE 37*
Prospero Frazzini & Brothers
Italian-American Bank
Denver, Colorado
Photographer unknown
Date unknown
15⅛ x 20 inches

Prospero Frazzini opened the Banca Popolare Italiana, later renamed the Italian-American Bank, on 15th Street in Denver in 1892. Frazzini became a wealthy and prominent businessman and was elected to the state legislature. In 1925, following a large investment in a company that went bankrupt, the bank closed, and Frazzini pleaded guilty to charges of embezzlement and grand larceny of bank funds. He died in prison in 1926.

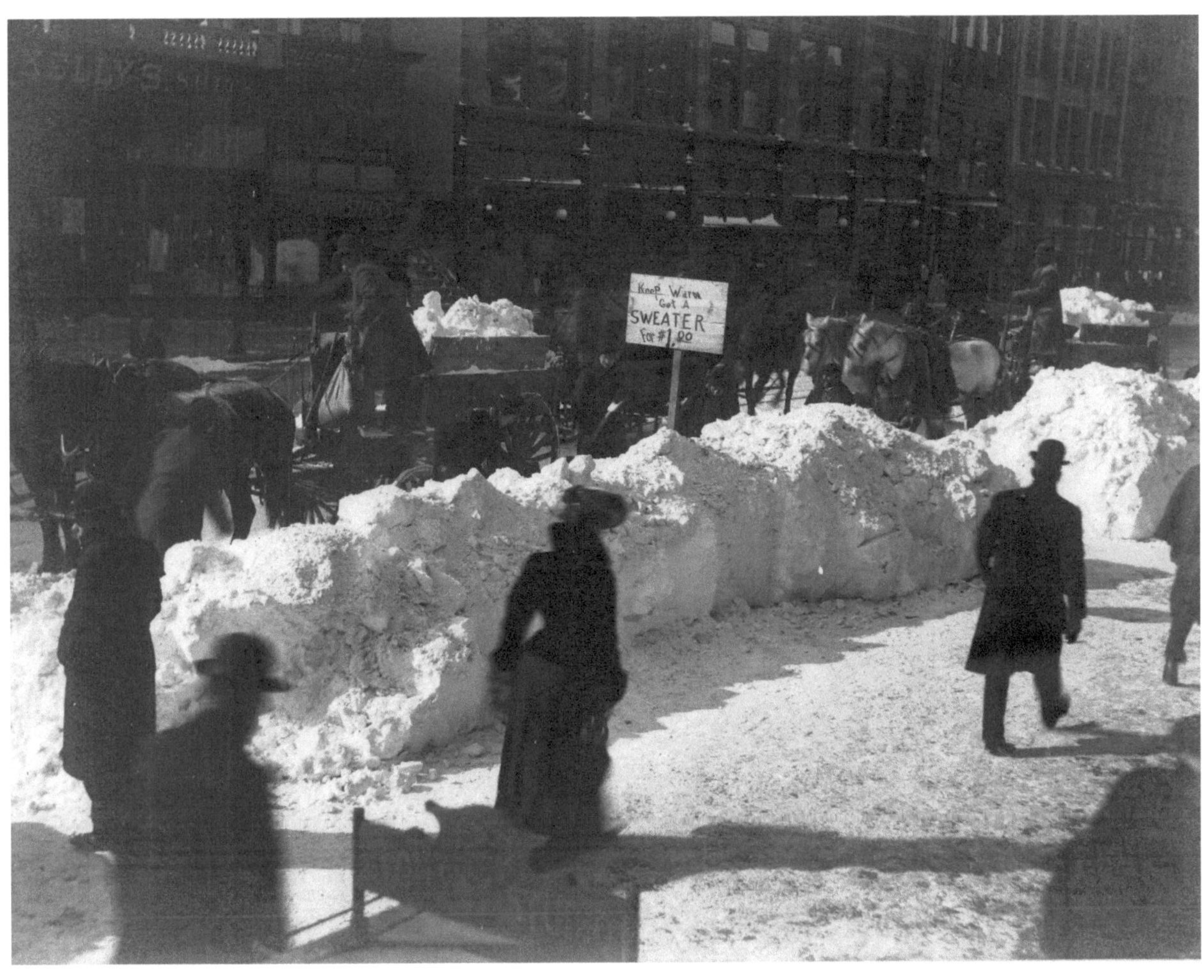

FIGURE 38
"Snow Removal/ Gli Italiani occupati nello sgombero della neve/ Sgombero della neve coi carri" [Italians employed in clearing the snow/ Clearing the snow with carts]
New York, New York
Photographer unknown
Date unknown
$10\frac{3}{8}$ x $13\frac{1}{2}$ inches

Judging from the store signage, this appears to be West 125th Street in Harlem, with the Koch Building (132–140 West 125th Street) and the Ludwig Baumann furniture store (144 West 125th Street) in the background. The latter address currently houses the Studio Museum in Harlem.

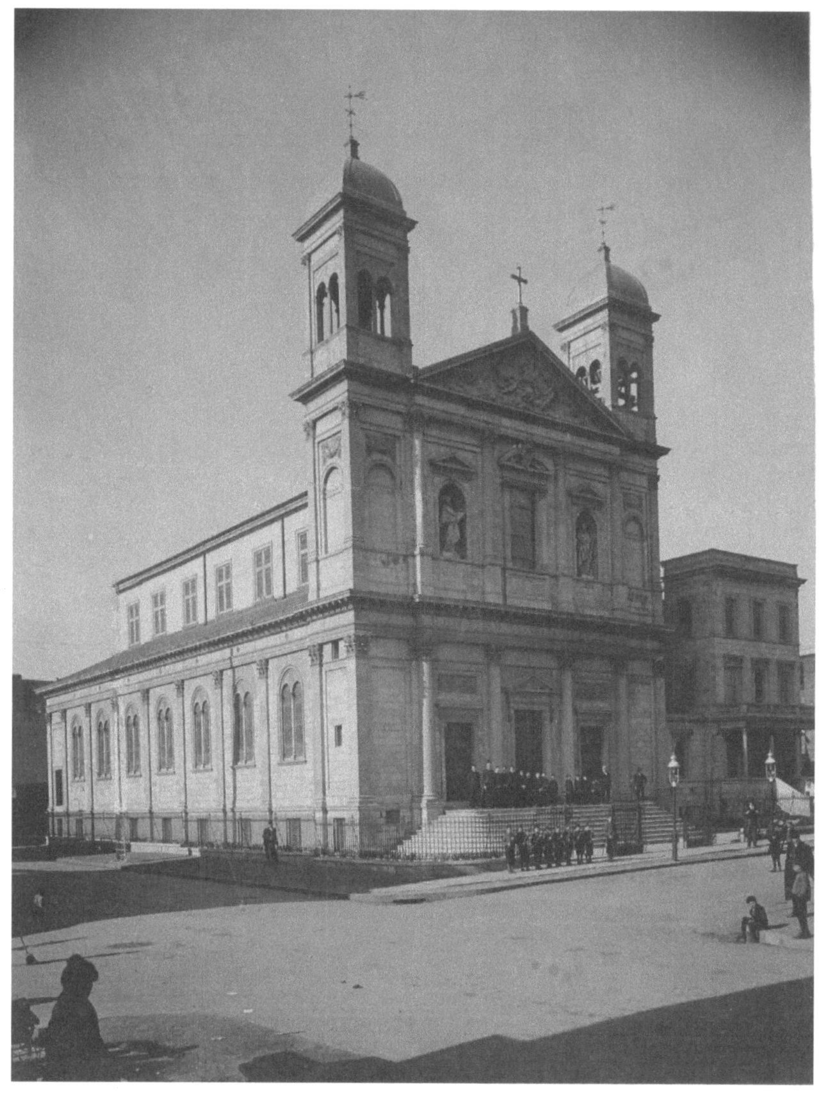

FIGURE 39*
Church of Our Lady of Loreto
East New York, Brooklyn
Photograph by Frank De Maria, New York
Date unknown
$7^{3}/_{4}$ x $6^{1}/_{8}$ inches

Architect Adriano Armezzani partnered with builders Antonio Federici and Sons of Paterson, New Jersey, to construct Our Lady of Loreto Church from 1906 to 1908. Gaetano Federici, Antonio's oldest son, was the sculptor for the building. The church was the subject of controversy beginning in 2008 when the Diocese of Brooklyn announced plans to demolish the structure and lease the land for the construction of affordable housing. Although a group of Italian Americans advocated to save the church from demolition, no definitive plan has been worked out as of spring 2015.

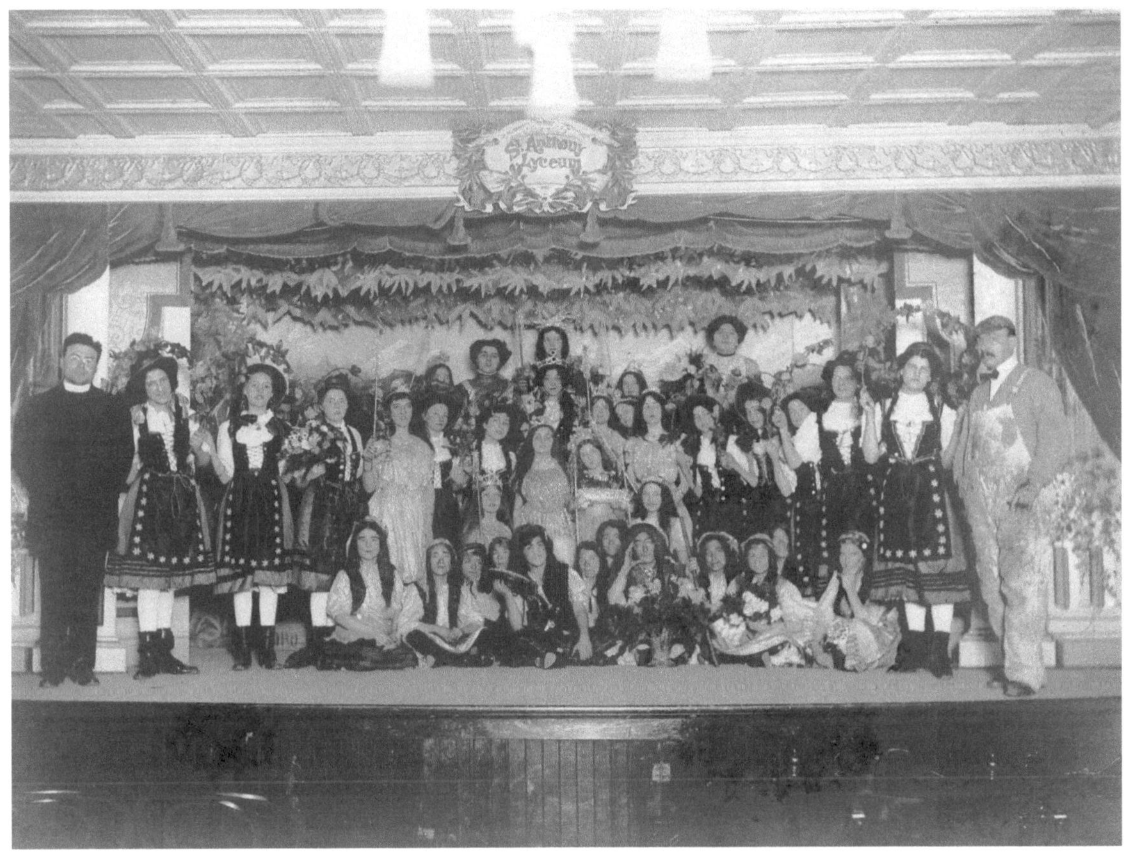

FIGURE 40
Basement of St. Anthony's Church,
Van Nest, Bronx, New York
Photograph by M. Goldberg,
New York
Date unknown
6½ x 8½ inches

The parish of St. Anthony's Church was established in 1908 to serve the Italian-American community. Construction of the church at 1496 Commonwealth Avenue was completed in 1909.

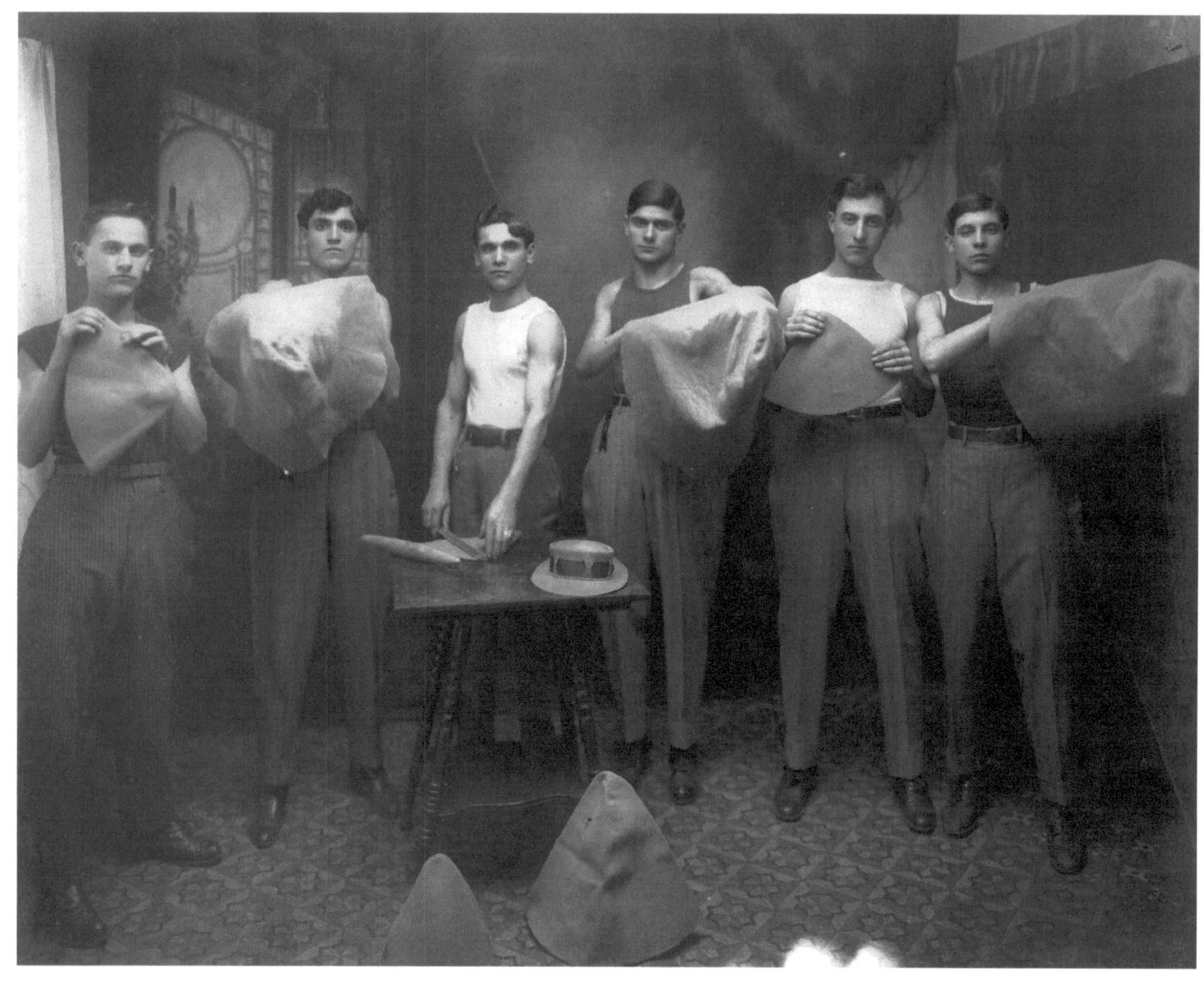

FIGURE 41*
"Gruppo Cappellai Italiani"
[Group of Italian Hatmakers]
Philadelphia, Pennsylvania
Photographer unknown
Date unknown
$10^{5}/_{8}$ x $13^{1}/_{2}$ inches

Afterword

John Turturro

WHEN JOSEPH SCIORRA invited me to write something about the photographs in this collection, which had been dropped off at the Calandra Institute in a suitcase with very little contextual information, I was intrigued. I'm a big fan of photography and use it in my research as an actor and director. Some of my favorite photographers are Saul Leiter, William Eggleston, Milton Rogovin, Lewis Hine, Murray Smith, Nan Goldin, and Jeanloup Sieff.

One photo from the collection that caught my eye right away is titled "Group of Italian Hatmakers"(Fig. 41). Five men hold up the felt used to make hats. Some pieces are large and unformed, while others have already been cut. A finished hat sits on a table, the proof of their hard work.

I'm not sure of the time period, but it can't be later than the 1920s, when men's hats were common. It used to be that what kind of hat you wore said a lot about who you were. When you think about a hat on a head, you get into the idea of it as a crown: It can add mystery, humor, shade, and finish off whatever style you have, or lack. I have some beautiful hats, but I never wear them. I prefer caps; they go better with my more modern head.

These six guys seem like they don't have a lot of money, and it looks like some could be related. What their lives were like, and the difficulties they encountered we'll never know. I'm sure they worked long hours, without a union. It seems to be hot in the place they're in, since they're all wearing T-shirts, yet they're wearing dress pants, wide at the hips and pegged at the bottom.

Another photograph. A school in Sunnyside, Arkansas, 1911 (Fig. 6). Children of Italian immigrants who desired to be educated. Probably many of them were southern Italians, and here they were in the deep south of America, far from where they had come. I'm struck by the seriousness of the children's faces. None of them smiling, all the boys in hats, the girls in pigtails, beginning their journey to becoming citizens of America. When I look at it I wonder about how many people spoke English, how fluently, or not.

Another photograph that caught my attention is of a third-grade class in a missionary school of the Sacred Heart in Scranton, Pennsylvania (Fig. 22). It looks like the 1920s because of the haircuts. The boys are wearing ties and jackets, and the girls are all in dresses, in the old

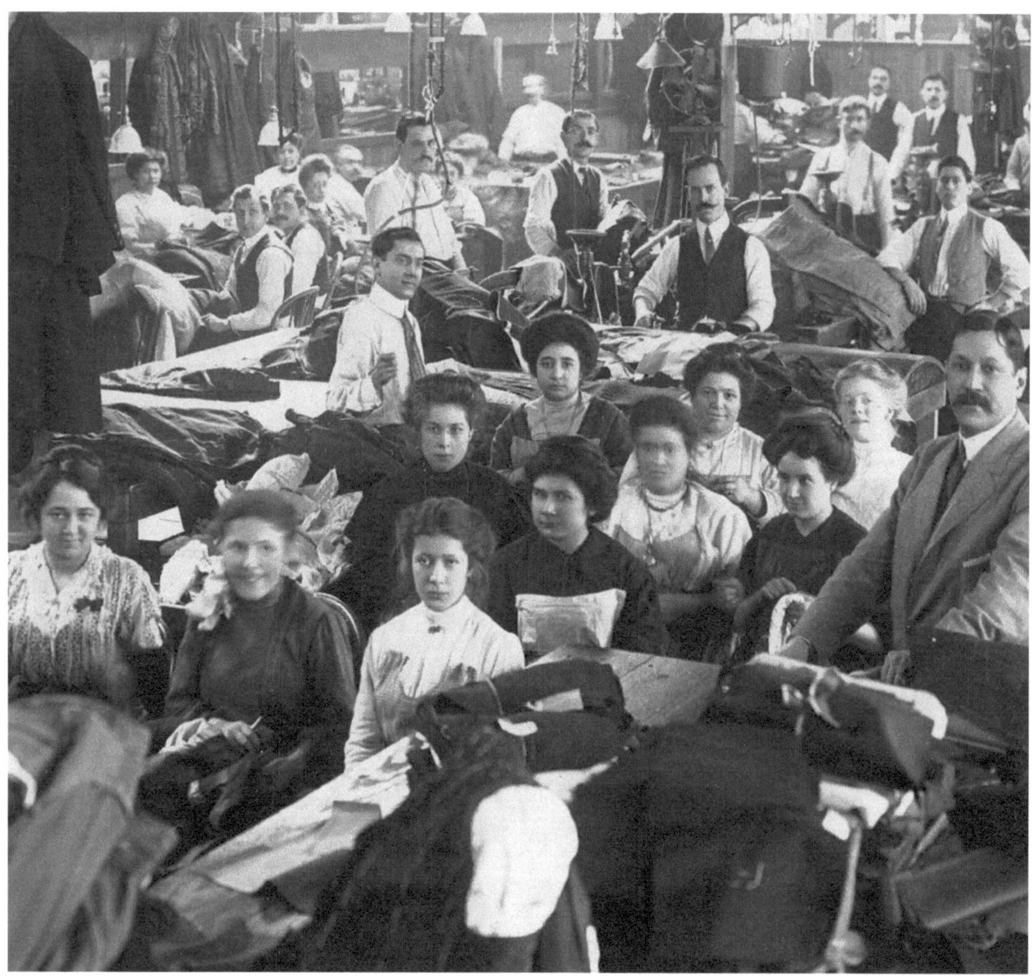

Detail: Snellenburg Clothing Factory

Catholic school tradition: Everyone is dressed like an adult, whereas today everyone is dressed like a kid.

When my father came to this country at the age of six he didn't speak any English, so they sat him up at the front of the class. It was a new world for him, coming from Giovanazzo, a small town on the coast of Apulia. He'd never seen a black person before, or a movie. The first film he saw starred Tom Mix, and he thought the horse was going to jump out of the screen, a precursor to 3D.

I'm reminded of my mother when I look at the photo of the garment workers (Fig. 17). Like so many other Italian Americans, my mother comes from this world, as do her cousins and one of her brothers—he actually became a supervisor. My mom's goal was to be a designer, and she got close (but she had to quit school because of the death of her own mother). She was taken under the tutelage of a German Jewish family, but they didn't have enough room to keep her in the business, which would have been her "finishing school." She continued making dresses for people and later in her life made dresses and wedding gowns on her own. The sewing machine was a big part of our lives growing up. She lost a lot of her vision beading skirts. Sometimes I would help her cut the pattern, or sometimes even model the gown and help her hem it, since I was tall and skinny.

Nobody is smiling in these photographs, and that's what I like about these old pictures. You get a chance to see what they're thinking about, without having to look at their teeth.

Who knows how long each of these people lived? Who knows what their lives turned out to be, or if they ever got out of those schools and those factories? What we do know is that we are the beneficiaries of their sacrifice.

Contributors

ROSANGELA BRISCESE is Assistant Director for Academic and Cultural Programs at the John D. Calandra Italian American Institute and the managing editor of the Institute's journal *Italian American Review*. She is the co-editor of *Graces Received: Painted and Metal Ex-votos from Italy* (2012). Briscese received her MSIS from the University of Texas at Austin's School of Information, where she specialized in archives and preservation. She sits on the board of trustees of the Flow Chart Foundation (which oversees poet John Ashbery's archives and collections), the board of the New Jersey Folk Festival, and the Juglaris Publication Commission.

DOMINIQUE PADURANO is an independent scholar who writes on issues of Italian-American history and culture as well as ethnicity, gender, consumer and visual culture, and education in the United States. Padurano received her PhD in History from Rutgers, The State University of New Jersey, in 2007 and has taught at the University of Texas at El Paso, Long Island University, the Horace Mann School, and elsewhere. Padurano lives in New York City and directs Crimson Coaching, a private tutoring company that serves students of all ages across the tri-state area.

JOSEPH SCIORRA is Director of Academic and Cultural Programs at Queens College's John D. Calandra Italian American Institute. He is the editor of the social science and cultural studies journal *Italian American Review* and *Italian Folk: Vernacular Culture in Italian-American Lives* (2011), co-editor of *Embroidered Stories: Interpreting Women's Domestic Needlework from the Italian Diaspora* (2014), *Graces Received: Painted and Metal Ex-votos from Italy* (2012), *Mediated Ethnicity: New Italian-American Cinema* (2010), and the author of *Built with Faith: Italian-American Imagination and Catholic Material Culture in New York City* (2015).

JOHN TURTURRO is a Brooklyn-born actor and director. He has appeared in more than sixty films, including *Do the Right Thing* (1989), *Barton Fink* (1991), and *The Big Lebowski* (1998). In 2013 he starred, with Woody Allen, in *Fading Gigolo*, which he also wrote and directed. He took part in the landmark PBS documentary series *The Italian Americans* (2015).

www.ingramcontent.com/pod-product-compliance
Lightning Source LLC
LaVergne TN
LVHW070141110826
845147LV00002B/301

* 9 7 8 1 9 3 9 3 2 3 0 7 1 *